Facing Danger in the Helping Professions
A Skilled Approach

Iain Bourne

 Open University Press

Open University Press
McGraw-Hill Education
McGraw-Hill House
Shoppenhangers Road
Maidenhead
Berkshire
England
SL6 2QL

email: enquiries@openup.co.uk
world wide web: www.openup.co.uk

and Two Penn Plaza, New York, NY 10121-2289, USA

First published 2013

A catalogue record of this book is available from the British Library

ISBN-13: 978-0-33-524583-3
ISBN-10: 0-33-524583-8
e-ISBN: 978-0-33-524584-0

Library of Congress Cataloging-in-Publication Data
CIP data to come

Typeset by Aptara, Inc.
Printed in the UK by Bell and Bain Ltd; Glasgow.

Fictitious names of companies, products, people, characters and/or data that may be used herein (in case studies or in examples) are not intended to represent any real individual, company, product or event.

Facing Danger in the Helping Professions
A Skilled Approach

Praise for this book

Written for professionals who may experience violence in the course of their work, this book is – unusually – not about helping the violent person become less violent (worthy though that goal undoubtedly is) but about helping the professional to be safe. In this, it is a welcome addition to the literature on social work. Social workers, nurses, care staff and others are often expected to work in tense, fraught situations in which emotions can run high. This book is unique in offering practical tips to help guide professionals in responding to threatening and violent behaviour.

David Wilkins, Honorary Lecturer, Centre for Child Protection Studies, University of Kent and Principal Child and Family Social Worker, London Borough of Enfield.

In the paramedic world during a typical inner city shift we face the unexpected, the hostile, the extreme and the bizarre in increasing numbers as a daily occurrence. We cannot remove all danger but we can reduce our risks and build strategies to ensure we are ready to sign off at the end of the shift and head home. Make sure you read this book and grasp the de-escalation tips and safety strategies it offers, and thereby ensure that you live to fight another day.

Bob Fellows (BSc) FCPara, Senior Paramedic Tutor

Contents

List of Tables

List of Figures

Chapter One

The Instant Aggression Model
The Language of Violence

In this chapter you will:
- gain an overview of different forms of violence and aggression
- learn about the different forces that drive aggression and violent behaviour
- distinguish between difficult behaviour and dangerous behaviour
- learn about the different pivotal points involved in reactive, disturbed and proactive aggression
- discover how these different strands combine in the Instant Aggression Model (IAM)

Consider the following scenarios:

You're working in a psychiatric ward when a patient, who is clearly psychotic, walks towards you wielding an iron bar accusing you of being in league with Satan . . .

You're on your way to a home visit when a passerby suddenly pulls out a knife and tells you to hand over your briefcase, wallet and phone . . .

You're in the reception area of your office when an agitated customer, who has been kept waiting, explodes with anger, kicking the chairs over and screaming at the receptionist . . .

A Foreign Language

While each of the above examples is an act of violence, they are quite clearly not the same. In fact there are so many variables and possibilities that you would not be alone if you were to conclude that every situation is different and you won't know what you can do until you are in that situation. Of course, if I were to agree with that premise there really would be no point to this book other than to cast a little more light on a very dark subject. That may be a worthwhile enterprise, but it is not what I have set out to do. My aim is to provide a guide to the helping professional in the handling of behaviour that may be difficult, disturbing and dangerous. It is for you to determine the extent to which this is achieved, and for the academics to scrutinize and challenge the underlying assumptions. For that reason, I will begin by spelling out here what those assumptions are.

In order to learn how to face danger skilfully, it may be helpful to draw an analogy with the process of learning to speak a foreign language. As it happens I have been trying to learn Spanish for some years, with limited success. Nonetheless, let's follow the analogy:

1 At first all Spanish and all Spanish people sounded the same, incomprehensible high speed verbiage with lots of rolling 'r's and lisping sounds. In the same way, at first all violence is thought to be one thing, all the same.

2 So I decided to learn about this strange tongue by trying to learn Spanish equivalents to English words. The task was overwhelming, particularly for an ageing man who no longer has as many grey cells as he once had. In fact it quickly became apparent that even if I knew the meaning of every single Spanish word, I still would not be able to speak or understand Spanish. Similarly, even if I knew everything there is to know about violence I might still be no better at dealing with it than the kid down the street. My first job was working in a therapeutic community for 'disturbed' adolescents – a terribly pejorative phrase referring to young people who been handed a bad deal and were now telling us about it. I had higher level degrees and qualifications and yet when things kicked off these untutored young people seemed light years ahead of me. My experience suggests that the practising professional does not have the time to learn every detail of the language of violence and that is not the approach I am taking here.

3 Then I tried learning phrases, which was okay if all I wanted to say was '*dos cervezas por favor*' and it gave the illusion of being able to speak some Spanish but, in fact that is all it was – an illusion. The truth was the *camarero* would have understood my order whatever language I spoke in, including sign language. Furthermore, if he had even come back with the most basic enquiry '*de barril?*' I would have been thrown into blind panic. In the language of violence, tourist phrases are the gimmicky titbits of advice offered everywhere from the school playground to professional training courses ('Don't show fear', 'Stay calm', 'Shout fire!' and much worse). I am not decrying these snippets just as I wouldn't criticize '*dos cervezas por favor*' – I am just saying that this shouldn't be equated with understanding the language, or that their utility extends beyond the most basic of encounters.

4   Next I decided that I'd have to learn some grammar and this was truly illuminating because now I could see that there were patterns and structures that would help demystify the language. I was good at this and could happily conjugate verbs all day long – I also enjoy playing chess and solving Sudoku puzzles. Now at last, I felt I had some mastery. Unfortunately, in conversation as opposed to pen and paper exercises, I turned out to be no more competent than my fellow tourists. The conversation starts, I decipher the first conjugated verb 'iremos' (to go), it is in the future form and refers to 'we' so I establish that it means 'we will go' – unfortunately by the time I have worked this out the speaker is several sentences further on and I am totally lost. When dealing with violence this is not a situation we would welcome and if you think Spanish is spoken fast, violence speaks a lot faster. This is not to say that learning grammatical structures is unhelpful – in fact it is essential to the learning process – I am simply saying that it is not the same as speaking the language. Similarly in the language of violence, we should understand the underlying theories, but that is not the same as understanding an act of violence *as it occurs*, even less how to respond to it. I can read in Spanish okay, because I can do it in my time – it's the real-time conversations that leave me behind.

5   Actually when speaking English, I never think about the grammatical structures I use and in conversation I don't listen to every word being said. Instead I pick up 'a sense' of what is being communicated. I recently attended an interesting lecture by an eminent professor and she was a fascinating and very eloquent speaker. Afterwards I remembered the general theme of her presentation but actually very little of the detail. I did vividly recall, however, the way she would blink frantically when (I am guessing here – but to my mind there was a very strong correlation) she was saying something contentious – and indeed those were the few points I remembered and the points that were subsequently picked in the questions from the audience afterwards. This didn't happen because we were all computer brains hanging on every word, critically analysing the content. Unlike my attempts to learn Spanish, I was for the most part 'zoned out', not listening particularly hard, but actually getting the message. It seems to me that the language of violence is a bit like that. We are actually quite good at 'sensing' what is going on and yet very poor at being able to understand the detail.

What Kind of Language?

I grew up thinking that most of the other kids were a lot cooler than me, and they knew how to handle 'stuff'. Somehow, I seemed to have missed that particular lesson and it put me at a great disadvantage and I felt very lonely. It was only a lot later that I started discovering that many of the people I assumed had got it all worked out were as much in the dark as I was. Even now I am constantly surprised, whether working with people who have lived a life of violence or the staff who work with them, that even these 'experts' appear to be little further on than I am with my fumbling Spanish.

As it turns out there are lots of languages of violence already to be found in the literature and I will briefly review these now before outlining the model proposed here. The purpose is not to establish an absolute truth, or even to find the most accurate model. That may be the task for researchers and academics but our purpose is to find a 'snap' model that can be used by professionals, second by second, when facing danger. In effect what we are looking to develop is the art and science of influencing another person's (or other persons') behaviour, immediately. That is, when confronted by a service user, who for whatever reason looks like they could cause us harm, how we exert an immediate influence over that behaviour. We are not talking about a therapeutic process or treatment paradigm whereby they will eventually learn to relinquish violence – we are talking about now, this time. For this reason I am calling it the Instant Aggression Model because it is about the violent act as it happens.

Approaches to Behavioural Change

Following our language analogy we are looking to learn the rapidly expressed and fast-changing spoken form of the language rather than its grammatically correct written form. In this context many of the traditional psychological theories about behavioural change fall short for one or more of the following reasons:

- They refer to slow behavioural change over an extended time span while we are interested in rapid change over a very short time span.
- They focus on the needs of the service user while our focus is on the needs of the helping professional.
- They assume a detailed level of information and analysis that the helping professional will rarely have access to during the incident.
- They are written to help us understand the behaviour rather than help the person faced with that behaviour.

A brief review of these contemporary approaches may help make the point.

Behavioural approaches suggest that if a specific behaviour or sequence of behaviours are rewarded or reinforced they will continue or be repeated. If they are not rewarded or reinforced, they will be repeated less frequently and eventually extinguish. This approach underpins much of what we do, from training dogs to managing the behaviour of children – indeed it seems to be the principle underpinning 'the naughty step' in popular TV programmes like *Supernanny*. I have no doubt that a consistently applied programme of behaviour modification will result in behavioural change, but the problem is that the change is slow and non-linear. Ignoring an irate service user is not only likely to be ineffective in the short term, but could lead to their behaviour becoming even more extreme. This is both because the act of ignoring the behaviour may make them feel devalued and humiliated, and because they haven't yet learned that their current strategy is ineffective and so may pursue it with even greater vigour.

Many readers will have undertaken training in cognitive-behavioural therapies (CBT), or at least have a passing awareness of these approaches to behaviour change. In very crude terms, the idea is that if you can change the way people think about themselves, others and the world, then their behaviour will change also. I have no argument with these approaches either, except that once again the process of behaviour change is slow and not anything like as specific as we require for our purposes. So we need something faster. I recall earlier in my career being strongly influenced by a book called *Change* by Watzlawick et al. (1974) and the subsequent writings that came out of the Brief Therapy Center in Palo Alto. As the title of their book and their centre suggests, they were interested in doing therapy briefly and sometimes very briefly, given the fact that many patients fall out of treatment after the first or second session. It is very clever stuff, but it's still far too slow and requires a very sophisticated knowledge of the patient's past attempts to address the presenting problem. The problem with violent behaviour is that the attacker does not usually invite us to change their behaviour, while another is that they may also be quite unknown to us.

Imagine . . .
You are investigating a possible child abuse case and, while visiting the family in question, an irate man bursts into the room and threatens to assault you. You have never seen the man before, you have no idea who he is, why he is so angry or what he wants. It is only after the event that you discover that he is the child's uncle (who you weren't even aware existed) and he is the one who has been abusing the child. Hindsight is a wonderful thing, but violence happens in real time.

The existing literature on behaviour change throws very little light on these fast-moving crises. In truth, there is probably very little you can know about the next dangerous encounter that you might face as it will occur:

- in a different place;
- under different circumstances;
- with different people involved;
- underpinned by different processes.

In fact, there is only one thing that you can predict about the next time you have to face danger and that is that *you* will be there. Everything else is a variable and so there is little point in worrying about all the other things that probably will never happen when the only guaranteed thing is that you will be there. Before we can manage someone else's behaviour we have to be able to manage our own and this will be the focus of Chapter 2.

Theories of Aggression

One of the earlier theories of aggression was proposed by Dollard et al. (1939) who argued that any sort of frustration inevitably leads to aggression. In a similar way Lorenz (1966), an ethologist, regarded aggression as inherited fighting instinct and considered that the suppression of aggressive instincts in human societies allows these natural instincts to build up, sometimes to the point where they are released in explosive violence. Bandura (1977) carried out studies with children suggesting that aggression is a socially learned behaviour that occurs through modelling their behaviour on others who they see being rewarded for acting aggressively.

Each of these theories has practical applications: the incidence of violence in A&E might be reduced if waiting times were kept to a minimum; sport might prove to be a way of safely channelling pent up aggression; children need positive role models. The problem is that while these kinds of theories might explain how to minimize the potential for aggression and violence in our societies, they do not give us much of a clue about what to do in the instant when aggression and violence spill over.

Anderson and colleagues (Anderson and Bushman 2002; Anderson and Carnagey 2004; Anderson and Huesmann 2003) argue that these theories are too simplistic and do not account for many types of aggression. Instead they advocate a more comprehensive approach to explain the diversity of aggressive and violent behaviour. Out of this came the 'General Aggression Model' which characterizes any aggressive act according to each of four dimensions:

- **automacity** – the degree to which action takes place spontaneously and without thought;
- the degree of hostile or agitated affect;
- the degree to which the primary goal is to cause harm vs. benefit the perpetrator;
- the degree to which the consequences are considered.

This is a fairly sophisticated model drawing on much of the work of social, personality, cognitive and developmental psychologists (e.g. Bandura 1977; Berkowitz 1989; Huesmann 1988; Mischel and Shoda 1995) since the 1970s. It would be difficult to do justice here to this model without going into much more detail – and therein lies the problem once again – it's simply not sufficiently intuitive or fast enough for our purposes.

Driving Behaviour

Even if we can learn to manage our own behaviour when faced with danger, is there any way that we can cut through the massive amount of data coming from the aggressor that will help us channel our resources effectively? In Chapter 2 we will consider the way in which it is possible to make very fast and accurate snap judgments in a crisis – judgments, in fact, we are making all the time. My fingers can move around this keyboard faster than I am able to think of the correct spelling of the words I am typing, for example. I can drive my car through central London while apparently (and frighteningly) giving virtually no thought to the vast array of complex and critical judgments I am making on my way. None of this, however, is untutored – I learned to type and I learned to drive. This is where the problem comes in when we need to make fast judgments when faced with violence. Most of us will never want, or be advised, to put in the hours of practice to master the skill of dealing with violence. The trick, therefore, is to find some short cuts and here we enter into the world of **rapid cognition** or the art and science of snap judgments. We will look into this in more detail in the next chapter, but the point about making snap judgments or using intuition is that these are only effective if they are based on extracting a '**thin slice**' of 'relevant' information – otherwise we are simply talking about prejudice.

So what is that thin slice of relevant information when it comes to violence? Although when confronted with threatening behaviour many people will ask questions – 'what do you want?' 'what's happened?' 'why are you doing this?' 'how can I help you?' – this is unlikely to be a fruitful path for the following reasons:

- In many cases the assailant may have very little insight into their immediate behaviour and, in asking them to explain themselves, we might be asking them to do something that they are unable to do. The last thing we want to do is to pressurize or humiliate them.
- Even if they understood their behaviour, they may be too wound up, too embarrassed, or simply unwilling to articulate it.

- Therapists strive to uncover the undercurrents that might explain their clients' behaviour and yet, with time on their side, may still be left fumbling in the dark. Is it reasonable then to believe we can uncover the truth behind another's behaviour in the terrifying moment before our impending destruction?
- Indeed, even if we absolutely understood the assailant's violent behaviour, it doesn't necessarily mean that we will know how to respond.

Exercise
In Chapter 4, there is a detailed description of a violent episode (pp. 83–87). Read through it and then ask yourself, honestly, how sure you are about how you would handle it. Then read Donna's story, which explains why she suddenly became so violent and it should begin to make a bit more sense. Now ask yourself again whether you are any better prepared to handle it more effectively.

My guess is that, knowing the back story, you might have a few more ideas, but the truth is you don't need lots more – you need one idea, right now, and the ability to act on that idea. After the incident, of course, understanding what triggered the violence may be very helpful, but during the crisis this may be nothing other than a distraction.

Drivers of Aggression

I'd like to propose a 'real-time' model that reflects the way in which we come into contact with dangerous behaviour and the way that many of us will intuitively sense what we are dealing with. The first point to make is that violent and aggressive behaviour is dynamic – it changes by the second. If it were static it wouldn't be frightening at all because we would have all the time in the world to study it, seek advice and consultation and formulate a carefully considered plan of action. It is precisely because we don't have the time to study it, as it happens, that leads us into terrifying and panicked states of **confusion**. Consequently our focus should not be on why the aggressor is behaving the way they are – that may be for ever a mystery – but on what might drive that behaviour to become even more dangerous. If we could know that, there is a possibility that we could do something about it. Here I propose that one of three forces might drive the behaviour:

- an emotion – usually an unpleasant one;
- a cognition – usually a disturbed one;
- a goal – usually a self-centred one.

Our interest, however, is not in the drivers themselves, but in the behaviours they generate. Following the terminology found in the existing literature I call these:

- **reactive aggression**
- **disturbed aggression**
- **proactive aggression**.

See Figure 1.1.

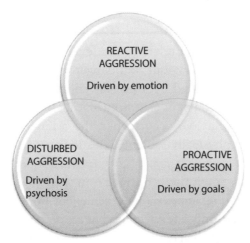

Figure 1.1. Three Drivers of Aggression

It would, however, be overly simplistic to suggest that these forms of aggression often occur in their pure form – the truth is that they often co-exist and overlap. It is clearly possible to be angry, hallucinating and determined to leave hospital all at the same time. At any moment, however, I would argue that one of these drivers will be predominant and that will be the one on which we must focus.

Examples of the drivers of aggression

Reactive aggression A resident sees another resident being given what they consider to be preferential treatment by the staff. It feels unfair and as they brood upon it their anger rises. Within moments they are striding towards the office in an angry and agitated manner hurling abuse at the staff.

Disturbed aggression During a case review, the service user's eyes dart around the room looking suspiciously at the assembled professionals. They begin to rock back and forth holding their hands over their ears. Suddenly they grab the social worker by the hair screaming 'I know who you really are . . . !'

Proactive aggression On a home visit, as the staff member enters the lounge, they notice the service user's partner watching child pornography on the television. The partner walks menacingly towards the staff member, pushes them against the wall while quietly issuing threats of violence against the staff member and their family.

The next part of the model refers to the level of the behaviour and distinguishes between **difficult behaviour** and **dangerous behaviour** which exist on a continuum, but are separated by a **pivotal point**. Difficult behaviour as the name suggests refers to behaviour that is escalating but has not yet turned into violence. Dangerous behaviour occurs when the behaviour develops a force of its own and becomes physically violent. Let's look at some of the differences (Table 1.1).

The pivotal point is when the behaviour is in the balance and it feels that it could go either way and separates difficult behaviour from dangerous behaviour. These moments may last only a few seconds but are absolutely critical, because at these points the aggressor's behaviour is highly changeable and that could place us in great danger, but it also gives us some hope of transforming that behaviour.

Table 1.1. Distinguishing Difficult and Dangerous Behaviour

Difficult behaviour	Dangerous behaviour
The aggressor still exerts a reasonable amount of control over their behaviour	The aggressor's behaviour becomes driven predominantly by one of the three driving forces
Although the behaviour becomes increasingly difficult to manage, and may be escalating, it is not yet dangerous	The behaviour may already have become physically violent, or at least feels like it could become violent very easily
The person dealing with the behaviour still has time to think about how best to handle the behaviour	The behaviour is escalating so rapidly that there is no time to think

I have called these points the **dysphoric crisis** (reactive aggression), the **psychotic crisis** (disturbed aggression) and the **psychopathic crisis** (proactive aggression). These will be described more fully in the next section.

Despite the new language here, it is my experience that helping professionals can usually spot the difference between these forms of aggression intuitively and immediately without training. That is, most of us can tell fairly easily if a service user is angry/upset, or disturbed, or on a mission to cause harm. In the same way most of us can sense pretty much immediately when behaviour is rapidly escalating and when the aggression is being acted upon. I am also convinced that for the most part, we can spot the pivotal point, the point where we hopefully under our breath, might let out an expletive. I call this an intuitive model because, although some of the language may be new, for the most part we can rapidly navigate our way around it without having to think. Let's have a closer look at each form of aggression.

Reactive Aggression

Undoubtedly this is the form of aggression that helping professionals and indeed the general public are likely to come across most often. This behaviour is usually associated with high levels of arousal and is normally driven by an unpleasant emotional state, although less commonly it may be driven by euphoria (cf. mob violence) or sadistic excitement. Generally it occurs when the aggressor feels wronged and it's not difficult to imagine a whole range of circumstances where service users may feel this way. They may, for example, feel:

- powerless in the face of what they see as a decisions made by professionals about their future;
- frustrated by endless bureaucracy;
- angry because they feel unfairly judged;
- fearful about the outcome of an investigation.

References to reactive aggression abound in the literature: Holtzworth-Munroe (2000) reviewing battering studies refers to this as dysphoric-borderline aggression; Babcock et al. (2000) looking at domestically violent husbands refer to it as affective violence; Pulkkinen (1987) in a study on juvenile offenders refer to it as defensive aggression; Monroe (1978) studying the behaviour of aggressive criminals calls it episodic dyscontrol; Barratt et al. (1991) in a pharmacological study refer to it as impulsive aggression; and finally Berkowitz (1994) among others actually calls it reactive aggression.

Several keys points come to mind in considering reactive aggression.

- From the viewpoint of the helping professional knowing how to respond to Reactive Aggression will be the most important because even in incidents that are being driven by a psychological disturbance or a goal, the moment where the behaviour spills over from aggression into violence will most often be triggered in a state of heightened arousal. Knowing how to manage those sudden emotional eruptions (Chapters 3, 4 and 5) will, therefore, be critical.
- Although there are many adherents to the catharsis theory ('it's best to let them get it out of their system') there is little evidence to support this. Indeed Bushman et al. (1999) found that letting off steam actually increased the amount of aggression. Obviously there may be a place for therapeutic catharsis which may prove effective when the person can safely express or release low levels of pent up emotions, but this is quite different from the uncontained expression of rage. Indeed it is my experience that once even quite small levels of disaffection are expressed *towards someone*, the aggressor often finds it difficult to know how to withdraw and so ends up painting themselves into a corner.
- As the level of emotion rises to the pivotal point, the aggressor will find it increasingly difficult to articulate their concerns, problem-solve or even remember what made them so angry in the first place. The Yerkes-Dodson Law (Yerkes and Dodson 1908) shows how levels of arousal affect performance differentially according to the difficulty of task. Simple, routine tasks (e.g. running) are performed best at high levels of arousal while more complex tasks (e.g. those that involve thinking) are impaired (see Figure 1.2).

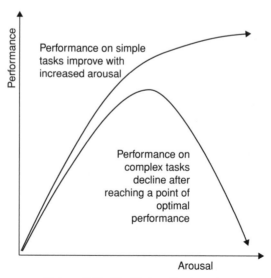

Figure 1.2. The Yerkes-Dodson Law

The point at which the aggressor fails to express themselves effectively through words is also the point, therefore, that they may begin to express themselves physically. In Chapter 5 this will be explored further and in relation to reactive aggression I am calling this 'the dysphoric crisis'. It is the point where the aggressor loses their internal map of where they are going and what they are doing. It is a moment that may feel like an eternity when they may feel exposed, humiliated and under intense pressure to act. It is as if a vacuum or chasm opens up before them and the only way to survive the moment is to do almost anything to fill it – perhaps in the hope that if they can buy time, they might find a way to regain some control.

Not all emotion is the same. Greenberg and Safran (1987) distinguish between primary emotions and secondary emotions. Primary emotions are those that we feel first in response to a specific cue. Consider the following example:

> In a case conference the chairperson belittles a suggestion you have made. In response you feel angry so anger is the primary emotion. The anger alerts you to the fact that this is a situation that you should do something about. However, imagine that you have been brought up to believe that it is not acceptable to show anger. Then you might feel embarrassed or ashamed – these are secondary emotions.

So secondary emotions are those we feel in response to the primary emotion and they tend to last a lot longer and are generally less helpful to us. The primary emotions are fear, joy, love, sadness, surprise and anger – although love and joy, for obvious reasons, are rare companions of aggression, while sadness and surprise are less often the cause for aggression than fear and anger. To

Table 1.2. Primary and Secondary Dysphoric Emotions

Primary dysphoric emotions	Secondary emotions (and related tertiary emotions)
Fear – a survival mechanism that alerts us to that something bad is about to happen	Nervousness (anxiety, apprehension, distress, dread, tension, uneasiness, worry)
	Horror (alarm, fear, fright, hysteria, panic, shock, terror)
Anger – a response to (perceived) ill treatment	Rage (fury, loathing, hate)
	Irritation (agitation, aggravation, bitterness, resentment, frustration, exasperation)
	Disgust (revulsion, contempt)

further complicate matters, there are also tertiary emotions, but rather than get bogged down in this I have listed the dysphoric (feeling bad) emotions in Table 1.2. So fear and anger are the primary emotions implicated in reactive aggression and these have physical correlates within the body, which is why we sometimes call these 'feelings'.

Disturbed Aggression

While reactive aggression and the driving effects of unpleasant emotions predominate, sometimes, particularly when working with people who exist in conditions of severe duress, other more disturbed forces can propel the behaviour. Disruptions in our cognitive worlds (delusions and confusion) and perceptual worlds (illusions and hallucinations) can begin to take hold of a service user's behaviour. This may be due to a psychiatric disorder such as schizophrenia, induced chemically through the misuse of drugs, a result of brain injury or disease, or triggered at times of enormous distress such as abuse or bereavement.

The media often have a field day with this and the tabloids in particular never appear more joyful than when they can splash 'Psycho Killer!' headlines across their front pages. The truth is that the vast majority of people troubled by mental health issues are anxious, depressed, withdrawn, lacking confidence and would never dream of hurting anyone other than themselves – and are far more likely to be victims of violent crime. In fact Fazel and Grann (2006) studied 13 years of data from Sweden, where population data on mental health and crime is kept, concluding that: 'In many ways the most interesting aspect of our findings is that 19 out of 20 people committing violent crimes do so without having any severe mental health problems' (http:/news.bbc.co.uk/1/hi/health/5216836.stm). So the link between mental health issues and violence is tenuous at best and we should really worry about the other 75 per cent of the population that are perpetrating 95 per cent of the violence. That said, as helping professionals we tend to work within populations in which a much higher proportion of mental health issues and substance misuse exists, and in circumstances where loss, bereavement, abuse and trauma are frequent bedfellows.

While the literature provides strong support for a bimodal classification of human aggression (McEllistrem 2004) based on what I have termed here reactive and proactive aggression, the prevalence of temporary, episodic and ongoing mental health issues within the caseload of many helping professionals marks disturbed aggression as an important and central concern. The media scare stories, along with inadequate mental health training, can leave many helping professionals feeling deskilled when faced with this kind of aggression.

After all, most of us will have had some firsthand experience of reactive aggression, if not in our professional lives, at sometime in our personal pasts. Not everyone, however, has had to deal with disturbed aggression and often our biggest fears are of the unknown.

As indicated earlier, it is possible, even likely, that a person experiencing such massive disruptions will also be experiencing enormous fear and anger. The question is, whatever triggered the aggression, what is driving it right now? Consider the following:

> Mr. Jones arrives at your office in an angry and agitated state clearly unhappy about the service he and his family has received. Before coming, however, he takes Ecstasy thinking this will help him. As he bursts into the office, everyone suddenly stops talking and stares at him. Mr. Jones looks around wildly and interprets the fact that people have stopped talking as evidence that they were all talking about him before his arrival. The growing sense of paranoia is further reinforced by the fact that everyone is staring at him. Within seconds he is hurling furniture about and screaming, 'Stay away from me!'

Clearly this incident started as reactive aggression and yet in the end, at the critical moment, it was the disturbance that was driving the behaviour. The staff might try to calm Mr. Jones down, but if Mr. Jones sees them as conspirators, this is unlikely to be effective. Instead, the immediate task is to deal with the paranoia and this along with other forms of disturbed aggression is the focus of Chapter 6.

As indicated in the previous section, the converse can also be true. Consider the following:

> You are visiting a service user who is in the later stages of dementia. You are aware that their mental health has been deteriorating rapidly but as you enter their room you are nonetheless shocked to find them frantically trying to reach out at something non-existent. Their failure to grasp the imagined object is clearly frustrating them and as a result they start picking up objects and hurling them around the room.

In this case presumably the dementia has affected the visual cortex resulting in visual hallucinations. However, the aggression is not being driven by those perceptual disturbances, but by the frustration at not being able grab hold of whatever they believe they are seeing. Consequently the focus should not be on the hallucinations but on the rising frustrations.

Proactive Aggression

Here we are referring to aggression that is goal driven and purposeful and has also been referred to as 'predatory' and 'instrumental'. Consciously or otherwise, the service user has calculated that aggression will result in a desired outcome. I guess in some way we could call all forms of aggression goal driven – consider the examples below:

> A resident becomes highly abusive to staff in order to convey how distressed they are.
>
> A patient in a psychiatric ward starts banging their head against the wall because they want the voices to stop.

In both cases the behaviour would appear goal driven, but in neither instance would we consider the behaviour to be an example of proactive aggression. There are a number of factors that make proactive aggression quite distinct. First, whereas with both reactive and disturbed aggression the goal is proximal – that is immediate – with proactive aggression the goal may be distant. Contrast the above examples with this one:

> You are at work on the night shift in a forensic unit and you have noticed a recent change in the atmosphere. There is a knock on the office door and a couple of residents enter carrying baseball bats and tell you to hand over the keys to the drugs cabinet.

Unlike the previous examples, here the aggression had a strong element of premeditation. The aggressors weren't caught up in the chaos, emotion or disturbance of the moment – they knew what they were doing and the goal wasn't to frighten the staff member but to gain access to the drugs cabinet. The aggressors had decided before the incident that the best way to get hold of the drugs was to threaten violence, but if they thought it would be easier to bribe the staff member that would have been their course of action. Consider another example:

> You work with women escaping from domestic violence. One day you get a call from a man who turns out to be the ex-partner of one of the women you are supporting and he wants to talk to you. You know that he has repeatedly and violently assaulted his partner in the past. He says he realizes he needs help but doesn't know where to turn.

Obviously the sensible thing here would be to decline his invitation but to signpost him to agencies that could help him. It is interesting, nonetheless, to speculate on who this man may be and what his motives are. Naturally, he may have genuinely recognized that he has a problem that he cannot solve by himself and is therefore seeking help – although one might wonder why, of all the people he could have approached, he chooses the person who is still in contact with his ex-partner. Two other possibilities are supported by the research. In a study by Babcock et al. (2000) violent and non-violent husbands were compared and categorized according to their level of attachment to their partner – secure, preoccupied or dismissive. They then labelled the violence as either expressive or instrumental, which equate to what we are calling here reactive and proactive aggression – and no surprises, those perpetrators who were preoccupied with their level of attachment exhibited reactive aggression, primarily in response to a fear of abandonment. Those that were dismissive of their attachment to their partners on the other hand, tended to engage in proactive aggression (or as they called it predatory or instrumental violence) as a means of asserting authority and establishing control over their wives (see Table 1.3).

On that basis, we might assume in our example that the caller was the type who finds it difficult to establish secure attachments and becomes violent when fearing abandonment. There is a problem, however, because proactive aggression unlike

Table 1.3. Attachment and Violence

Secure attachment	Pre-occupied attachment	Dismissive attachment
Non-violent	Reactive aggression	Proactive aggression
Healthy relationship	Aggression driven by fear of abandonment	Aggression driven by a wish to assert control authority and establish control over partner

Source: Babcock et al. 2000.

reactive and disturbed aggression is slow burning and the goal can be carefully hidden. What if his apparent desperation is a masquerade and all the time he is plotting to reclaim his ex-partner into his controlling lair? This would appear to cast a cloud over the intuitiveness of our model – people who engage in proactive aggression are often also good deceivers. That, however, would be a misunderstanding of the **Instant Aggression Model** (IAM). This is a model to guide us through what is happening *right now as the violence or aggression is taking place*, and when faced with proactive aggression, I can assure you, you know it! What the model can't tell us about is the planning, scheming and subterfuge that lures us into a web of violence. For this reason, in Chapter 7 we look beyond the immediate crisis to establish ways of working safely with high-risk service users.

The Role of the Autonomic Nervous System

What about the behaviour itself? How is Proactive Aggression manifested so differently from the reactive and disturbed forms of aggression that you would know it? One obvious and glaring difference is the role of the autonomic nervous system which is essentially responsible for the regulation of our internal organs and glands. The nervous system is divided into two parts, the **sympathetic nervous system** and the **parasympathetic system**. The sympathetic nervous system is associated with the **acute stress response** (the fight-flight-freeze response, see Chapter 2) and corresponds to increasing levels of arousal – in a motoring analogy it would be the accelerator. The parasympathetic nervous system does pretty much the opposite, promoting a calming response – effectively it acts like the brakes of a car. As you may have guessed reactive and disturbed aggression are closely linked with the activation of the sympathetic nervous system, while proactive aggression is closely associated with activation of the parasympathetic nervous system. Many of you will have cats, so that might provide a useful and observable analogy.

Imagine a new cat arrives in your garden and your cat experiences a sudden threat to its territory. It reacts – its hairs stand up, its tail fluffs out and its back arches making it look larger. Its breathing becomes louder and it may hiss and growl while it unsheathes its claws. That is the sympathetic nervous system at work and the cat is reacting to a threat. Now compare that with when your cat is stalking a bird or a mouse – most overt signs of the sympathetic nervous system are absent. Instead the cat takes up a predatory stance, it goes quiet and lies low to avoid detection. When the attack occurs, instead of using its claws, it attacks with its mouth to the head or neck and is more precise in delivering a series of deadly blows.

Of course my cat would never do such a thing – I am simply referring to the observations of Wasman and Flynn (1962)! Although we should be wary about drawing conclusions about human behaviour based on animal studies, I think the analogy is clear in this case. Chapter 6 will look into the human analogues of this predatory behaviour in more detail. Before we move on, however, we should note that this is not the exclusive domain of predators and psychopaths. In football do we want our strikers to go for goal, no matter what, or would we prefer that they consider the feelings of the opposition goalkeeper first? If we are waiting outside in the cold for the new year's sale hoping for a real bargain, when the doors open are we really going to allow everyone else to go in first, or might we push ourselves past others to get what we want? And who among us has never thought about gaining revenge on someone who has crossed us?

More on Pivotal Points

The astute reader will have notice that up to this point I have used the terms aggression and violence rather loosely and made little reference to the levels of that behaviour. Consider the example below:

> During a contact session between a mother, father and their son, the father turns to you saying, 'I've had a guts full of you lot pushing me about and I'm telling you there is only so much I can take.' He goes silent, his face reddens, he bites his lip, clenches his fists and his breathing becomes heavier. His wife turns to him saying, 'If it weren't for you we wouldn't be in this bloody mess!' Suddenly he gets up and pulls her by the hair . . .

Clearly everything changes dramatically at the point when he gets up. Prior to that point the father was becoming increasingly agitated and was showing signs that he was having great difficulty with the developing situation. Also the professionals in the room at that time might be experiencing a growing sense of alarm and would probably be wondering how to prevent a further escalation. In this example the pivotal point is the moment just prior to the father rising from his seat. If nothing is done he might well reach the pivotal point without any further prompting. His wife's interjection, however, acted as an accelerant bringing him to that point much earlier. The rules operating in that room prior to the eruption are very different to those operating after. There are two major differences following the pivotal point:

- the speed at which events take place accelerates exponentially;
- the level of arousal of everyone in that room also rise dramatically.

Prior to the pivotal point the professionals could think how to best deal with the developing situation; afterwards the events take place faster than they can think. This is important because it demonstrates that we cannot talk meaningfully about aggressive behaviour without referring to the level at which it is occurring.

A number of points arise out of this observation:

- In dealing with difficult behaviour (i.e. prior to the pivotal point being reached) we can use skills in the traditional way – we can think before we act. These are the **defusing skills** and **de-escalating skills** explored in Chapter 3.
- At the pivotal point, the crisis is in the balance and is unlikely to remain at that point for very long. It can be likened to performing a balancing act in a storm.
- At the pivotal point, the aggressor's behaviour is not difficult to change, but highly changeable. Although we may concentrate on all the factors that could lead to the situation worsening, it is important that there are just as many factors that could lead to an improvement.
- At the pivotal point the professional will no longer have any time to think and will have to act instantaneously – these are the rapid reaction skills explored in Chapter 5.

I have already described the dysphoric crisis, the psychotic crisis and the psychopathic crisis as the three pivotal points. Each of these can be understood in terms of a **force-field analysis** or the balancing of restraining forces and driving forces (Lewin 1943). The driving forces have already been identified as negative emotion, psychological disturbance or a goal. In relation to difficult behaviour these driving forces are kept in check by restraining forces such as:

- protection of their own self-image – violence may involve a loss of control leading to embarrassment, humiliation and shame;
- fear and anxiety about the unknown – how will others react, will they be able to carry through with their own aggression?
- self-questioning – are they really sure that this is the best course of action?
- social norms and injunctions – violence may be at odds with assimilated social expectations about what does and does not constitute acceptable behaviour;

- a negative appraisal of their chances of achieving a successful outcome;
- awareness of the unintended effects of their aggression – for example noticing frightened bystanders;
- awareness of the consequences that will follow the behaviour.

At the pivotal point, these and other restraining forces are exactly in balance with the driving forces of rising emotions, disturbance or determination. With dangerous behaviour, the driving forces override the restraining forces.

The Instant Aggression Model

The IAM (see Figure 1.3) aims to help us map out where we are and what we are dealing with at any point when faced with aggression. It proposes that at any point

	REACTIVE AGGRESSION	DISTURBED AGGRESSION	PROACTIVE AGGRESSION
DRIVING FORCE	An unpleasant emotional state	A disturbed cognitive or perceptual state	A goal
LEVEL 1 DIFFICULT BEHAVIOUR	Increasing levels of agitation and arousal	Increasing loss of reality and self-control	Increasing need to use threats, intimidation and coercion
PIVOTAL POINT	The dysphoric crisis	The psychotic crisis	The psychopathic crisis
LEVEL 2 DANGEROUS BEHAVIOUR	Highly reactive, largely out of control violent behaviour	Highly disturbed violent behaviour largely controlled by hallucinations, delusions and paranoia	Violence chosen as a means to a clear end

Figure 1.3. The Instant Aggression Model

one of three forces will be driving the behaviour, and these are an unpleasant emotional state, a psychological disturbance, or a goal – and that it is possible to know this intuitively and with little need for thought – at least once we know what to look for. These driving forces are counter-balanced by restraining forces, such as self-image, social norms, fear, expectations and consequences. As the driving forces escalate the level of aggression reaches a pivotal point which differs according to whether the aggression is reactive, disturbed or proactive. The pivotal point is the point when the aggression is in the balance and could either suddenly tilt towards violence, or return towards safety. These pivotal points are called in turn the dysphoric crisis, the psychotic crisis and the psychopathic crisis. These do not refer to any form of psychiatric diagnosis but to the form of behaviour being displayed at that specific moment.

This is the language that we will be using to navigate our way through the rest of the book. Before we look at the skills, however, we need to consider our own reactions because it won't matter how skilled we are if we are paralysed with fear – so this is what we will explore in the following chapter.

Summary

We have looked at the three primary forces – a negative emotion, a disturbed psychological state, or a goal that drive aggressive behaviour – and these can result in what we have called either reactive aggression, disturbed aggression or proactive aggression. We also noted that the aggressive behaviour can be identified as either difficult or dangerous behaviour. Although these exist on the same continuum, there is a critical moment called a pivotal point where one transforms into the other. These moments may be brief but can result in massive shifts in behaviour. Knowing which force is driving the behaviour helps us identify where to focus our energies.

Top Tips
- Instead of trying to understand why a service user is becoming increasingly aggressive, learn to identify what is driving that behaviour – is it an unpleasant emotion, a psychological disturbance or a goal?
- Don't be misled by the service user's background – just because they may be in a psychotic state does not necessarily mean that the psychosis is driving the behaviour. It might be that even though they are hearing voices, the driving force is their sense of terror, for example.
- Remember that although violence can sometimes seem inevitable, there are often more restraining forces than forces driving that behaviour.
- If you can identify the driving force that is where you will need to direct your efforts to reduce the chance of them reaching a pivotal point.
- Try reviewing some of the aggressive episodes that you have experienced or witnessed to see if you can understand them in terms of the IAM.

Chapter Two

Managing Our Own Reactions
The Crisis Within

In this chapter you will:
- discover the importance of accurately reading signals that come from your body when under threat
- learn how your brain and body combine, both under normal circumstances and during a crisis
- explore the nature of 'Intuition' and the critical role played by the thalamus
- find out about concepts such as 'thin-slicing', 'survival schemas' and 'front-end rapid reaction skills'
- Clarify what you need to learn to face dangerous behaviour effectively

Imagine . . .

You're 9 years old and you have only recently started at a new school mid-term. Things have been difficult because you have no friends, and you stand out as different – different clothes, different accent, different everything. A group of older kids have been making your life hell. At first it was mostly name-calling but it wasn't long before they started pushing you around. Yesterday they took your lunchbox and your pocket money and were saying they were going to stick your head down the toilet. You are scared of them. They are bigger, more confident and there's at least six of them. You've never been in anything more than a play fight with your brother before. You have sleepless nights and spend fruitless hours searching for a solution. The trouble is that when confronted by these kids nothing ever comes out of your mouth. You are bright and at least you think you are cleverer than them – so how come your brain doesn't seem to come up with anything? Playtime is the worst; you try to find any excuse not to go into the playground.

One day you are in the playground thinking you had given them the slip when suddenly they surround you. The gang leader starts a chant, 'Toilet! Toilet! Toilet!' and now they are all joining in with the taunt and laughing at you. Suddenly you find yourself running at the gang leader. Incredibly he falls over and you find yourself on top of him pinning him down. He is screaming 'Get off me!' but he can't budge you. You are waiting for his mates to jump on you but strangely they don't appear to be doing anything. You look down at the boy who had been making your life hell and he is crying. You've won! You've beaten them! You should be jubilant – then you burst into tears.

Well that was my first inglorious experience of violence. I hadn't really thought about it much until I started writing this book. What strikes me most about it is that none of it was how I expected. The endless hours of rehearsal were irrelevant. All my assumptions about their size, confidence and numbers meant nothing – and when against all odds I emerged victorious, I blew it all by bursting into tears. We can speculate about the tears – tears of joy, of relief, of shock maybe. It seems to confirm what participants often say at the beginning of my courses – 'every situation is different' or 'you'll never know until it happens to you' or 'no amount of training will prepare you for that moment' or 'the rules are out the window'. Now while I have to admit that there is a certain amount of truth in what they say, if I were to accept that fully, this would be a very short book!

It's Not About Them!

Let's go back to the story. It is interesting to note that this really had very little to do with 'the gang' and everything to do with me. To this day, I can't say what was going on with my tormentors and most of my speculations at the time only made me feel more helpless. Even if I could have known their motivations and machinations and then have expert advice miraculously beamed into my brain, I would have been no better off if I froze, choked up, went blank, burst into tears or lashed out – just because we know what to do doesn't mean that we will be able to do it. Herein lies the fundamental point – the critical issues when faced with potential violence are not about our assailants, but about us.

In a crisis, and maybe in life, there is only one thing that we can hope to know, and that is what we experience – and that be very different from the experience of others. In any future crisis just about everything will be a variable – it will be in a different setting, with different people, at a different time, with different triggers and different underlying causes. There is only one thing that we can be sure of, and that is that we will be there. This has to be our starting point and it raises many questions:

- How do we know when we're in danger?
- How do we respond when threatened?
- What resources do we have?
- How do we uniquely affect others?
- How can we get our act together as the crisis hits?
- What happens in our brains and in our bodies?

Of course the service users are just as important and where appropriate I will include their story in the narrative – after all I guess we wouldn't be in the helping professions, much less likely to read this book, if we weren't interested in our fellow human travellers. Nonetheless, if we can't manage ourselves, we have no hope of managing the crisis that threatens to engulf us.

It is interesting to note how many books and practice guidelines begin, or have at their heart the principle 'remain calm'. Good common sense you would think, because if you lose the plot you are unlikely to be of much assistance to anyone. Being calm can clearly be a great bonus in many situations and I have no problem with advocates of 'low arousal' approaches for dealing with aggressive behaviour. However, keeping your head and remaining calm are not the same thing and I think that statements such as this set us off on a path that leads rapidly to a dead end.

Obviously in an ideal world we might hope to remain calm, but what if we are not? On some of my courses there is a dramatic re-enactment of a very violent episode and the participants, all helping professionals, are simply an audience. Nonetheless, many physically jump and some scream when it starts – even though they are told to expect it. They are not calm and telling them to be calm would not make them calm. If being calm is a prerequisite for dealing with violence most of us should stay at home! These are experienced, confident and competent professionals and if 'remain calm' is our mantra, this book will not be for them, you or me. Just as in my story, things just don't seem to work out the way you expect. Many people will report experiences where they were shocked by how calm they were in what should have been an absolutely terrifying ordeal yet fall apart over an apparently trifling matter. We cannot become calm by telling ourselves to be calm any more than we can be happy by telling ourselves to be happy. If our physical and emotional reactions followed verbal commands debilitating anxiety states could be resolved with the directive 'chill', or deep depression alleviated with the instruction 'be happy'. The second problem with mantras like 'remain calm' is that even if it were possible, being calm is not necessarily calming. Think of two people in a deteriorating relationship, where one partner is clearly very upset and angry with the other. Their partner tries to respond as calmly as possible only to discover that objects are now being thrown in their direction! Their attempt to be calm may have been read as arrogant, superior, 'not getting it', being unfeeling, or it may just make them feel stupid.

The problem is not with being calm or not, but with prescriptions that seem to take no account of the way our brains and bodies operate or the complex environment in which we might work. We react the way we do in a crisis for good reason and the last thing we want is a battle with ourselves. Just like when we lose our footing and slip, our brain and body do an incredible job of keeping us upright and none of this has anything to do with thinking, doing what we are told to do, or remaining calm. The trick is to find a way of responding that is consistent with the way our brain and body are intended to work, that neither provokes or inflames but rather contains the situation. The concern, however, is that if we don't remain calm, we may end up acting like I did in rushing at a 9-year-old 'gang leader' – and that would be highly unprofessional!

Acting Before You Think

Many of us, when faced with aggression will respond with questions to discover what lies behind the behaviour:

- 'What's happened?'
- 'Why are you behaving like this?'
- 'What do you want me to do?'

The assumption is twofold. The first that it is possible to understand 'why' another person is behaving the way they do in a moment of rage, while the second is that if we understood that behaviour we might be able to calibrate an effective and appropriate response. That is, if we don't understand what is happening, at least they might. I think both assumptions are flawed and are more likely to lead us to panic than an effective resolution. Often the reason that the other person is acting out is precisely because they don't know the answers to those questions and even if they did they may well be unable or unwilling to share it. Therapists can spend years trying to discover what lies behind their client's behaviour with variable success, so is it not somewhat arrogant for us to assume that we can find a short cut through this in split seconds as someone explodes in our face? Understanding is for later.

In my story, all those torturous hours spent trying to solve the problem got me nowhere. I have nothing against thinking and indeed much of my career has been devoted to encouraging professionals to reflect on their practice through supervision (Brown and Bourne 1996). Maybe as a 9-year-old if I could have taken the situation to supervision I might have found a better way of responding. However, in many of the situations that we will be looking at in this book it would have been difficult to anticipate what was about to occur, much less take it to supervision. To think before you act might be one way of defining professional behaviour and this begs the question – what happens when there is no time to think? Let's go back to our example of slipping and losing our foothold. Do you think 'What is happening?' 'How have I dealt with this in the past?' 'How should I best deal with this now?' I don't think so. More likely your body seems to take over and instead of thinking before you act, you act before you think. Thinking would be too slow. Obviously when we have time to think then we should do so taking into account our code of ethics, our organization's policies and procedures, the defusing and de-escalating skills in Chapter 3, the service user's needs and so on. The scary bit, however, is when we don't have that luxury. Is it possible to act professionally in a crisis when we have no time to think, and when our bodies start to take over?

The Acute Stress Response

So the problem with dealing with violence is that often we may need to act before we think – if only to duck the oncoming blow. This becomes frightening because if we can't put thought before action, how do we know if that action may not be wholly inappropriate and escalating? Beyond even that there is the fear that we may lose all control over our brains and bodies. We might panic, go blank or freeze, for example. It would seem, therefore, that any further exploration of this area would only be of academic interest. If our bodies react faster than we think, how can we know (for example) how not to freeze, when we didn't know that we were going to freeze until we froze – and then it's too late? Well I have been pondering on this conundrum for some time and if you will stick with me, I hope to show that there is light at the end of the tunnel.

The term 'fight or flight' was originally coined by William Cannon in 1929 and refers to what we now call the acute stress response which can be triggered in the body when faced with immediate threat. I say 'can be' because this is not the only response possible, as we shall see, although ethologists – experts in animal behaviour – have noticed that these are the major physical responses to threat found in the animal kingdom. Following from this a third body reaction, 'freeze', has been noted – and so the term fight, flight or freeze comes into usage. However, Bracha (2004) argues that while the acute stress response is consistent among mammalian species (including human beings) the correct sequence is freeze-flight-fight-fright, which at first sounds rather confusing as freezing would appear to preclude the options of flight, fight or fright. Although the sequence, originally described by Gray (1988) begins with what ethologists call 'the freeze response' or 'freezing' this is not the same as the state of **tonic immobility** (the body going rigid, playing dead) with which it is commonly associated. Instead he has identified it as a state of hypervigilence (being on guard, watchful or hyper-alert). To avoid confusion, I will refer to this preliminary state of hypervigilence as the **focussing response**, reserving the freeze response for its everyday meaning. As we will see in the next section this focussing response may be critical in our search for a professional path through moments of extreme stress.

The focussing response is immediately followed in the sequence by an attempt to escape, or the flight response. However, if this is impossible or attempts to escape have been exhausted, the next stress response in the hierarchy is to fight. Thus, 'flight or fight' is the proper order of responses rather than 'fight or flight'. Of course there is a question as to whether this holds true for human beings also – is our first reaction, after identifying the threat, to run? Actually I think it is, or at least that is what our bodies want to do. Psychologically we might want to believe that we aren't scared, or that we shouldn't show fear, or that we should stand our ground, or that we don't want to lose face – but at the same time our bodies are screaming at us 'Get out!'

Most professionals won't consider themselves to be violent people and yet when cornered – physically or psychologically – any of us could be just that. If you are a parent you might reflect on your response to the discovery that someone is harming your child – and I very much doubt that it will be flight. Sometimes, however, the fight response is not available or the body senses that fighting would be met with even more overwhelming violence and that the best chance for survival is not to resist. The next step in the sequence of fear-circuitry responses after fighting, therefore, is tonic immobility – or the freeze response in our revised terminology. A mouse cornered by a cat may 'play dead', and if I were parachuted into a war zone where people were shooting one another, I might just lie on the ground and pretend I was dead.

So Bracha (2004) proposes the adoption of the expanded and reordered phrase 'freeze, flight, fight, or fright' as a more accurate alternative to 'fight or flight'. Here we will refer to these stages as 'focus, flight, fight, freeze' in order to stay with the more commonly understood use of the term 'freeze'.

Emergency Psychological Processes

If all we are left with in a crisis is the acute stress responses of flight-fight-freeze then we are slaves to our fate. However, when I reflect on my own experience of critical incidents it occurs to me that there is rather more to it than just a physical and physiological response. At one point in my career I worked mostly with people who had experienced **type 1 traumas** (recent, sudden overwhelming events often leading to PTSD – as compared with **type 2 traumas** which involve ongoing, repeated, historic abuse) and these people would often report terrifying experiences in such incredible detail that it would be hard not conclude that, alongside the physical stuff, something of real psychological significance was also taking place. In this section, I am grateful to and draw heavily upon an article by Dyregrov et al. (2000: 73) in which the authors propose that alongside the acute stress response there 'is a similar system of mental mobilization that is activated in critical stress situations, enabling us to deal with danger in an optimal way'.

Normally in response to danger we tend to think of physical processes taking over from psychological processes. However, the emergency psychological processes as identified by Dyregrov and his colleagues would appear to occur not only prior to cognition, but also prior to the onset of the acute stress response. They occur at the very front-end of the crisis – at the point described in the previous section as the focus state. How they integrate with the acute stress response will, therefore be of great interest and importance. First, let's take a brief tour of these **emergency psychological processes**. Although Dyregrov et al. describe these processes as occurring simultaneously, logically some must occur before others. Staying with their analysis I will differentiate these processes as either focussing responses or processing responses.

Focussing Responses

These are the psychological states that kick in immediately as we sense or realize that we are under great threat and correspond to the first stage or step of the acute stress response. Dyregrov et al. (2000) describe these states as enhanced sensory awareness, focussed attention, altered time perception and deactivation of emotional responses.

Enhanced Sensory Awareness

Imagine you are doing the sleep-over in a children's residential home. You are the only one on duty when you hear a noise downstairs. You go to investigate but all the children are in their rooms. You can find nothing untoward but for the rest of the night it is as if you could hear a pin drop.

It seems that once we are alerted to danger all our senses become very acute, ready to pick up on the slightest cue. This is, of course, essential for our survival. In working with trauma clients it is amazing how much detail they picked up during the critical moments of their crisis. It's as if the brain is saying 'pay attention, don't miss a thing!'

Focussed Attention

Imagine being in a group setting when a client suddenly pulls a knife on you. Everyone else in the room drops into the background and all you can notice is the knife pointing at you. The knife appears very large and everything else recedes into the background.

Selective attention is clearly very beneficial in a life-threatening situation as it concentrates all our responses on the aspect of the crisis that will be most important to our survival. According to Solomon and Horn (1986) police officers involved in armed response incidents report a tunnelling around the critical aspects and an exclusion of peripheral details. It is also possible that some senses become more focussed on than others – in the example above, for example, the sight of the knife, or the look in the assailant's eye might predominate to the point that the screams and shouts of other group members are hardly heard.

Altered Time Perception

'He just suddenly went wild! He was throwing things about, accusing me of all sorts. He hit me and then I saw him holding a dirty needle. I was scared, scared for my life. There was murder in his eyes. He kept going on and on – I thought it would never end. I couldn't understand why no one was coming to help me. After a long time I began wishing he would just kill me and be done with it.'

This incident was caught on CCTV in an interview room. Officers were there within 30 seconds and yet the victim experienced this as if it were going on for ever. They were not lying or exaggerating, that is how they experienced the incident. Being objective is not necessarily helpful however – my computer is objective, but has no idea how violent I feel towards it when it stubbornly refuses to do what I want it to do!

This altered perception of time occurs for good reason and is our friend. It occurs first because we need to take in a far greater volume of information within a very short period of time than normally. This results in each moment feeling fuller and consequently longer. Additionally, violence occurs in real time and not reflective time – that is, when someone raises a fist to you, you don't know that it will dissipate to nothing in the ensuing seconds and so each second can feel like an eternity. In real time, you don't know when it will be over, until it's over.

Deactivation of Emotional Responses

> Think of the most dangerous situation you could imagine. How do you imagine you might feel? Terrified, shaking, a quiver of a wreck, a burbling incompetent?

You may or may not react in this way but things are often not as you expect. Violence is about the short process; trauma and therapy are about the long process. Maybe we need to reconsider our experience of violence. There are three phases to consider:

- Before: our fears about violence happening to us;
- During: our experience of violence as it happens to us;
- After: our reflections on violence that has happened to us.

All three dimensions are central to this book. At this point, however, I would like to focus on the point violence occurs rather than the preceding moments or the following trauma. For most of us, it turns out that this is the least scary moment:

- We might feel quite detached from it.
- It may not feel real.
- A calmness might come over us.
- We might be operating on auto-pilot.

The worst imaginable atrocity is actually happening, we should feel absolute terror . . . and yet somehow everything might seem quite surreal. Both worrying about what might happen and reflecting on what has happened can be terrifying. Actually when things happen everything can feel very different.

> A police officer involved in a gun battle described watching himself in slow motion shoot the perpetrator. He described how he felt devoid of emotions, yet well able to function. Another police officer that was shot described watching himself fall to the ground. He reported little pain and an ability to focus on keeping calm and surviving the incident.
>
> (Dyregrov et al. 2000: 75)

If these officers were filled with emotions at the point of danger, these might severely hamper their ability to channel their survival resources. Somehow, the (temporary) deactivation of their emotional reactions appears to allow us to activate a sequence of actions that were not thought out or calculated, but operate in auto-pilot. Indeed, in my low level story at the beginning of this chapter, when the violence happened there was no emotion – but lots preceded and followed it. How this occurs will become critical when we consider the rapid reaction skills in Chapter 5.

There is an important corollary to this and that is this deactivation of emotions is only likely to occur as long as we are doing something. Being passive during a violent encounter will probably leave us at the mercy of our uncontained emotions. Furthermore, experiencing intense fear, helplessness and horror at the time of the trauma strongly predict the development of PTSD afterwards (Brewin et al. 2000).

Processing Responses

The focussing processes provide us with at least a starting point in identifying or understanding the immediate psychological intake of dangerous information. These processes are there to help us – to take in information fast and to focus our resources where they are needed. Unfortunately all this information also has the capacity to confuse us and send us on misdirected courses of action. Among all the incoming data, how do we know what to pay attention to – and even less what to do about it?

The clues are found in the other emergency psychological processes (Dyregrov et al. call these 'Mental Mobilization Processes in Critical Incident Stress Situations'). These are:

- rapid processing of incoming data;
- enhanced memory;
- **state-dependent learning.**

These are more complicated processes to understand, but nonetheless ones that can occur instantly and more importantly drive responsive behaviour. Without these processes the Instant Aggression Model would require substantial revision. These processes refer to the seconds that occur at the pivotal points identified in Chapter 1.

Rapid Processing of Incoming Data

As I am writing this (April 2012) there are a series of reports on the news of soldiers returning from the Middle East receiving various medals for gallantry and bravery. Interestingly and consistently when asked by reporters what went through their minds as they were carrying out acts of remarkable heroism they replied along the lines of 'nothing really, I just went into auto-pilot'. Some said 'I guess my training just kicked in'. Somehow, these brave people were able to act rapidly and without apparent thought and yet their behaviour wasn't stereotypical – none of them had ever been in that self-same situation and learned to act in that precise way. Their behaviour was in response to what they were experiencing second by second – as if they were thinking without thinking. In fact, they were acting in many cases faster than they could think – thinking is a slow linear process involving words being put into grammatical sequences. Malcolm Gladwell (2005) in his popular book *Blink* reviews the way in which very accurate 'snap judgements' can be made in split seconds or a blink. He uses the 'theory of thin slices' or rapid cognition to explain this. He argues that past experience can enable us to distil enormous amounts of information down to a very 'thin slice' of information on the basis of which fast decisions can be made. As Gladwell shows, however, snap judgments can be incredibly good and incredibly bad – it all depends on whether you are able to 'thin-slice' the correct information. *Blink* is not specifically about violence so I will leave you to read it at your leisure. You may also be interested in the work of Gary Klein (2004) who has researched intuitive approaches to make better decisions.

The point, however, is not only that we should be able to take in information faster than we can think, but that we should be able to accurately 'thin-slice' that information and then activate an appropriate survival schema or rapid reactions. How this might occur will be explained in the final sections of this chapter.

Enhanced Memory

The first time we experience being under severe threat we may not have much of a template or mental map to guide us and we may feel quite lost. All of us, however, have had some experience of facing danger even though we may feel that we learned little from the experience other than how terrifying it can be. Each time we have these experiences, even though it might not feel like it, the contours of the crisis become clearer – we may not be able to think how this might be or to be able to articulate what our body has learned, but it has learned something. Sometimes that learning will help us and sometimes it will hinder us.

You are walking down a dark, narrow alleyway towards your car when a man grabs you by the throat from behind. He is trying to strangle you, but you can't see him. As you struggle you become very aware of the smell of nicotine on his breath. A colleague rushes to your assistance but the assailant escapes . . .

Following this you might very sensibly decide to avoid dark narrow alleyways. It might also be wise to avoid having anything more to do with this man if at all possible. Unfortunately, you didn't see him, you only smelled the nicotine on his breath. Logically you know there is no reason to believe that smokers are any more dangerous than non-smokers and yet every time you pick up that smell your body immediately tenses up. Your thought processes tell you one story while your body tells you something else. It is this kind of faulty learning that creates a problem for us when considering how to learn to react rapidly and effectively in a crisis. What if we react to a situation as if it is a crisis when actually it isn't – or more worry-ingly, vice versa? The way around this is to develop a way of responding to danger that is effective even if we had somehow misinterpreted the risk.

State-dependent Learning

Although I am reluctant to admit it, there is a problem with learning how to face danger through reading this book and that is that you could read it a hundred times over and learn every detail and indeed write a much better version of your own – only to forget it all as someone kicks in your office door. Afterwards, when you are lying in your hospital bed you might wonder why all that learning disappeared at the very point when you needed it most. This is because there is a constant inter-play between your brain and your body, each taking a cue from the other. If right now you are reading this book and your body is in a relatively relaxed state, your brain learns that this is information that you will need to recall when you are feel-ing relatively relaxed. When the door gets kicked in, presumably you will be in a rather alarmed state, and then your brain will recall what it learned when alarmed. This is called state-dependent learning. Imagine you go out for an evening with your friends, you have a great time and there's a lot of laughter and good humour. A friend tells you a story that you find so amazing that you resolve to remember it to tell everyone you know. Next morning you wake and to your amazement you just can't think what the story was about. However, two weeks later you are out having a good time with some other friends and to your astonishment you are able to recite the story almost word for word!

This is why the 'Difficult, Disturbing and Dangerous Behaviour' training pro-gramme is conducted as a kind of intense fringe theatre event. Participants may forget the training when back in the office writing up their case notes, but hope-fully next time, maybe many years later, they encounter a dangerous situation, all the learning suddenly kicks in. This book can tell you how to 'thin-slice' danger (i.e. spot it almost before it has happened) and what your body has to learn to do when faced with danger – it cannot however put you into a state where your body can learn to combine the two. Furthermore it is not advised that you go out searching for danger to seek opportunities to practise your skills! Fortunately, the defusing skills and de-escalating skills (Chapter 3) are on the same behavioural trajectory and if you can refine these in the lower level situations, then you might be somewhat better prepared.

Parallel Processes

Dyregrov et al. (2000) suggest that the acute stress response and the emer-gency psychological processes operate in parallel. I have no way of knowing the truth about this and researchers in years to come will no doubt be able to throw more light on this, but I'd like to suggest a slightly modified analysis of how these processes combine. If we take the immediate response to danger as being the focussing response, it does not seem to me inevitable that our body will go into flight-fight-freeze mode at all, but instead might go into a state of rapid reaction. One of the soldiers referred to earlier saw a grenade drop in some water in front of him. He did not run, he did not freeze, there was no one to fight, but he did rush towards the grenade, pick it up and throw it into a ditch. So it would seem that following the focussing response either we could go into the acute stress response *or* the emergency psychological proc-esses might take over activating a survival schema (an unconsciously learned survival programme) or rapid reaction skills (a trained set of behaviours). See Figure 2.1.

Putting It All Together

Of course we could leave it there but for me at least it is important that we under-stand not only what happens, but how it happens. In the chapters that follow I will be proposing not just a general approach to deal with dangerous behaviour but specific skills to deal with that behaviour. Of course it is difficult to research the efficacy of these skills directly – it would hardly be ethical to arrange controlled groups of helping professionals to be attacked and then analyse the skills used by

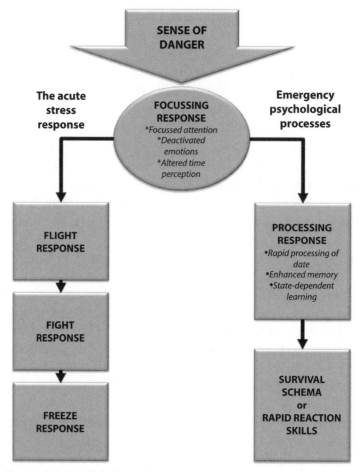

Figure 2.1. Parallel Physical and Psychological Responses to Danger

those who survived! However, it is important that any skills proposed are absolutely consistent with everything we know about how human behaviour operates under threat. In this final section of this chapter we will therefore review how our brains and bodies are hard-wired to cope with threats. The following is somewhat simplified, but here I am interested in the broad strokes rather than the fine detail. For those of you who wish to pursue these themes further I can highly recommend Debra Nierhoff's (1999) excellent book *The Biology of Violence*.

We can consider that the brain has three major sections (see Figure 2.2):

- the cerebral cortex – which we will abbreviated from now on to 'the cortex';
- the limbic system;
- the brain stem.

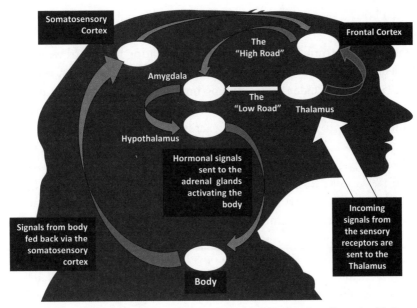

Figure 2.2. The Relationship between the Brain and Body when Faced with Danger

We won't preoccupy ourselves too much with the brain stem, important as it is for regulating autonomic functions such as breathing, heart rate, blood pressure and reflexes. These are all very significant when thinking about violence, but the brain stem is essentially the engine room and is controlled by the cortex and limbic system which are of more immediate interest to us.

The Intelligent Brain

The cortex is the largest structure in the brain and looks a bit like a large walnut. You can think of it as the brainy part of the brain specializing as it does in higher functions, thought, speech (receptive and expressive), complex motor actions, memory and so on. The importance of the cortex becomes apparent when it becomes diseased as in the case of Alzheimer's disease, or damaged through physical trauma or strokes (e.g. multi-infarct dementia). The deterioration in the cortical tissue leads to functional losses (amnesia – memory loss, aphasia – speech loss, apraxia – loss of complex movements, agnosia – loss of meaning, etc.). The **frontal cortex** is part of the brain's executive system responsible for planning, reasoning and judgment and this is the part of the brain that as professionals we are asked to exercise. Indeed as you read the words on this page, your front cortex will be trying to make some sense of it and making decisions as to whether or not you should read on! You can think of it as being like a computer, it's an information or data processor.

So far there's nothing very surprising or illuminating here until we ask how the cortex decides upon what information to process. On a computer, the computer operator (you) will decide this by making inputs via the keyboard or mouse. So if you are playing a video game and move the cursors, the computer will process that input and turn it into an avatar running across the screen, or if you are typing into a word processor as I am, the keystrokes become letters and words that are then spell-checked, paginated and saved.

In terms of inputs to the cortex we are talking about the sensory signals that are picked up by our sensory receptors, taste, touch, sound, sight and smell. There must be millions of these coming in every second (don't quote me) and I guess it's just like your computer – if you have too many programmes running at the same time, the computer hangs, it just can't cope. Indeed if you had to 'think' about the dryness of your mouth, the weight of your body on the chair, the touch of your clothes on your skin and a million other things as well as the words from this book, it would be impossible and overwhelming. So somehow there has to be a filtering system, something that will determine what to process or pay attention to, and what can be ignored.

The Lizard Brain

This is where the **limbic system** comes in. Colloquially the limbic system is sometimes called 'the lizard brain' because it's fast, reactive and rather less thoughtful than the brainy cortex. In this group of organs, there are four which will interest us – the **thalamus**, the **amygdala**, the **hypothalamus** and the **hippocampus** (not shown in Figure 2.2 but this lies close to the amygdala) – there are others but we won't worry about these right now. The thalamus can be thought of as the gateway to your brain and is responsible for selective attention. Here again, the computer analogy may help. Think of your frontal cortex as an e-mail programme. You probably get a fair amount of junk mail, so you have a spam filter to stop the rubbish from distracting you. As you use the software more and more it becomes better and better at filtering out the junk mail and allowing you to concentrate your resources on the important mail. Similarly, a newborn baby may have some difficulty figuring out what to pay attention to at birth, but over time it will learn to screen some things out and focus on others (the mother's breast, faces, etc.). The thalamus doesn't think what to screen out because it operates prior to cognition taking place – it learns to spot this difference between proper mail and junk mail, not to read it. The proper mail then gets sent to the frontal cortex to be processed and made sense of, while the majority of sensory inputs are classified as junk mail, remain unopened and are either thrown out or filed away somewhere.

So for you right now the junk mail (e.g. road traffic noises in the background) is filtered out by your thalamus which then sends the relevant sensory inputs (e.g. the words on this page) to the frontal cortex where they can be processed into letters, words and sentences which are then thought about. The frontal cortex having done this will then decide what happens next and may activate other parts of the brain.

This is how we would like to think we behave as professionals and it's all very Spock-like. Now imagine this. I am talking to you quite calmly about this, that or the other and you find it all fascinating. Your thalamus has identified what I am saying as proper mail and is sending it to your cortex to be thought about – when a brick crashes through the window. Suddenly your frontal cortex will have difficulty making sense of what has happened and your body might well react before you (your frontal cortex) realize what has happened. It is being asked to respond to more than just data. The brainy brain is too slow and is wrong-footed, while another part of brain takes over – at least temporarily.

Emotional Processing

Just as your computer, or Spock, doesn't deal with emotions very well, neither does your frontal cortex. This is the job for the amygdala, the emotional processing centre in the brain. Before we go further, however, we need to clarify what we mean by an emotion. The way I see it, any signal that enters the brain that prompts a physical change in the body is an emotion or e-motion. So if I am angry, I feel it in my body, if I am sad, I feel that in my body, if I am scared, I feel it in my body – that is why we call them feelings. Conversely, if my body does not react to the input, it may be information, data, a concept or idea, but it is not an emotion. It is the amygdala's job to identify the physical correlate to the input and this is learned through experience. It is interesting that the amygdala has been strongly linked with post-traumatic stress disorder (PTSD) (Brewin 2008) suggesting that during a traumatic event the amygdala may learn to associate a particular stimulus with a fear response. Maybe this is also why we all react differently in different situations – one person may be able to parachute out of a plane without apparent fear, while being scared of spiders, yet for another just the thought of the parachute jump would send them into a state of panic.

However, the amygdala doesn't 'think' about this, it just identifies how the body needs to change and then relays this to the hypothalamus. Essentially the body change may be no more complex than a change in the body's level of arousal. The hypothalamus can be considered as the connection between brain and body and is the cornerstone of the hypothalamic-pituitary-adrenal (HPA) axis. The hypothalamus, receiving the information from the amygdala, then sends hormonal signals to the adrenal glands which in turn will release adrenaline and cortisol – stress hormones – into the body at the speed and volume calculated by the amygdala. If the amygdala calculates that the danger is imminent and immense, the stress hormones will be released into the body fast and in high volume probably triggering the acute stress response. If the threat is less, the result may be a greater sense of readiness.

The effect of the stress hormones is to prepare the body for action. The muscles will tense up, heart rate will increase, breathing become faster and the pupils dilate, along with a range of other physical reactions (see Figure 2.3). These bodily reactions

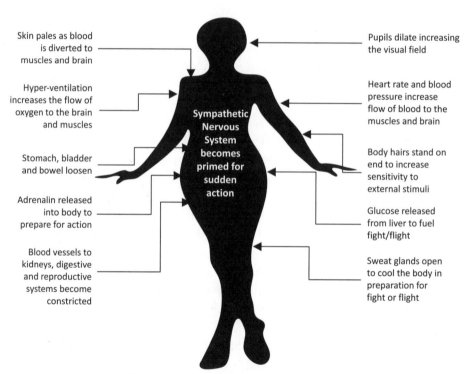

Skin pales as blood is diverted to muscles and brain

Hyper-ventilation increases the flow of oxygen to the brain and muscles

Stomach, bladder and bowel loosen

Adrenalin released into body to prepare for action

Blood vessels to kidneys, digestive and reproductive systems become constricted

Sympathetic Nervous System becomes primed for sudden action

Pupils dilate increasing the visual field

Heart rate and blood pressure increase flow of blood to the muscles and brain

Body hairs stand on end to increase sensitivity to external stimuli

Glucose released from liver to fuel fight/flight

Sweat glands open to cool the body in preparation for fight or flight

Figure 2.3. Physical Responses to Danger

are not something that we should try to avoid as they are there to help us deal with the incoming threat. If we try to change the way our body wants to go we will end up fighting with ourselves and probably panic. Instead the important thing to do is to make sure that we are able to channel these body responses. These are picked up by the somato-sensory cortex which is the part of the cortex that picks up what is going on in the body. Finally this information is then relayed back to the frontal cortex.

The Brain and Body

The frontal cortex then can put its initial crude assessment of the incoming signal 'Oh dear!' (or perhaps something more profane!) along with the new information from the **somatosensory cortex** – 'Look at the state of me!' – and then classify the experience by putting a cognitive label on it such as 'I'm scared', 'I'm angry', 'I'm confused', or whatever. Now the input becomes a concept that can be analysed in the frontal cortex – in a sense it becomes possible to compare this feeling of being scared, for example, with previous experiences of being scared, or indeed guidance about what to do when feeling scared. This is an expressible emotion, but the emotion itself was what happened in the body. This is interesting because the link between the somatosensory cortex and the frontal cortex is essentially about putting bodily reactions into words. The inability to do so is a condition known as **alexithymia** (a=loss or inability, lexi=language, thymia=feeling) which is a component on the autistic spectrum and has also been linked with increased levels of violence and aggression (e.g. Keltikangas-Järvinen 1982). Indeed this may also go some way to explaining some of the gender differences in the expression and response to violence.

Rapid Reactions

So now that we have the general picture we can move on to the really interesting bit and that underpins the rapid reaction skills in Chapter 5. The thalamus doesn't just filter in 'proper mail' and filter out 'junk mail', but it is also constantly on the lookout for danger mail- to use the email analogy, it also has an anti-virus function. Sometimes we have to act faster than we can think and sometimes we act without thinking. If we go back to the example of losing our foothold, some part of us must recognize that we are about to fall before we think about it, or we would end up on the floor – because thinking would be too slow to stop the fall. That part is the thalamus. Furthermore, once the thalamus spots a dangerous input, it must send it on a different route through the brain's executive system that by-passes the slow frontal cortex. This route has been called 'the low road' by neuro-scientists like LeDoux (1999) who suggest that the dangerous input goes straight to the amydala allowing much faster processing of the threat. In psychological terms this is the equivalent to **dissociation**, a state where the brain and body seem to act independently of one another. If you have been in a car crash you may have experienced this – often people talk of things appearing to happen in slow motion, almost as if it wasn't real. As another example, not related to danger, you may have experienced watching the TV only to realize that your mind must have been somewhere else completely because you have no idea what you were watching. Dissociation can also be a defence, a way in which the brain can protect itself from harm. Think of a child who is repeatedly sexually abused – while they can't avoid being there in body, they can take their mind somewhere else – they learn to dissociate. The point is, however, that the thalamus spots the threat before the frontal cortex starts thinking about it, and before the body responds. Although, as we saw earlier ethologists talk of the acute stress response in mammals as fight, flight or freeze – in human beings the fight and flight responses are not so clearly differentiated. We might, for example, when threatened start talking and moving rapidly out of a sense of survival to defuse the situation but no clear sense that we are in fight or flight mode. We could call this set of behaviours a survival schema – an automatic set of actions aimed at surviving a crisis. These survival schemas have either been learned unconsciously through prior experience or more overtly through training. This is where the hippocampus comes in – a part of the limbic system responsible for declarative memory which can be activated alongside the amygdala. Thus as the amygdala is activated directly, bypassing the frontal cortex it can nonetheless access the hippocampus and allow us to act on prior learning without need for thought. This is what the soldiers mentioned earlier described at acting on auto-pilot, or where they found their training kicking in – and this is where the rapid reaction skills reside.

However, few of us are in danger frequently enough to know what our survival schema is, or to have the opportunity to practise and refine it. That is part of the challenge for this book – to identify a safe, automatic, non-cognitive survival schema – or front-end rapid reaction skills. They are called 'front-end' because they are the skills you use immediately on encountering trouble, before you know what is going on, to allow you to take control of your body and contain the aggressor's behaviour – and they are called 'rapid reaction' because you have to use these fast and before you have time to think. Well let's say we can identify these front-end rapid reaction skills – isn't it still the case that we might well 'freeze' or 'lash out' before we can put them into action? And how can we stop ourselves from (say) freezing if we don't know that we are going to freeze until we are frozen – when obviously it's too late? Well here's the interesting thing – we don't 'know' in the cognitive sense of having thought it, but we probably can 'sense' it if only seconds before our body reacts.

Snap Judgments, Intuition and Rapid Cognition

Most of us have probably been in many situations where we had a 'sense' that something was not right, or a feeling that something was about to kick off. We could call this intuition, a seventh sense or gut reaction – or we could hypothesize that this is the thalamus doing the job it was designed to do from the day we were born. Gladwell (2005) describes an art dealer who goes into the Getty Museum where an ancient Greek statue, valued just under $10,000,000, is on display. The museum had gone to the trouble of having extensively tested to ensure it was genuine and yet immediately on seeing it, the art dealer declared it to be a fake – and so, following further extensive testing it proved to be. Gladwell doesn't mention how the brain could be capable of such a feat, but maybe that art dealer had looked at so many works of art over the years that her thalamus just recognized that something wasn't right. Because this was now interpreted as 'danger mail' it sent the information directly to the amygdala creating a 'feeling' which couldn't be rationalized or explained because the route was LeDoux's **'low road'** bypassing the frontal cortex. Another example in the book is of fire officers running from a building seconds before it is engulfed in flames, but not knowing what made them run. My guess is that if you are a fire officer, you get to sense the difference between a building which is safe and one which is not.

My experience suggests that most incidents are signalled beforehand, it's just that that signal may not be something that is that easy to articulate – and that might make it difficult to justify to colleagues, managers or service users. It might just be that it doesn't feel quite right, or there may be a churning in the stomach. It might also be that the signal comes only seconds before the violence breaks. On some of my courses there is a re-enactment of a violent incident by a homeless man. Afterwards most participants feel that the incident came out of nowhere, but when I remind them of what happened before the violence erupted almost everyone remembers and agrees that it was clearly broadcast – it's just that their time frame was much longer than the five second prequel. So there are two kinds of warning points – the first which might be the vague sense about a situation which should trigger a more cautious approach and more detailed risk assessment; and the second which may be the thalamus activating the limbic system for an immediate and rapid response.

In Chapter 4 there is a description of a violent incident involving a young woman called Donna. I have told this story to thousands of professionals and had the incident re-enacted before the groups. In the lead up, with all the time in the world, the groups are generally divided – virtually everyone senses that something is not quite right, but they usually disagree as to whether that is sufficient not to proceed with the visit. However, just about everyone knows that they are in deep trouble the moment they set eyes on Donna, seconds before she erupts. The fact that they know this unequivocally and almost instantaneously means that whatever told them they were in trouble, it wasn't a thought. Post-incident some participants rationalize it – blood, sweat, hyperventilation, dilated pupils, etc. – but in the space of one or two seconds there is no time for thought. It must have been the thalamus activating the 'low road'.

A Word of Caution

Finally, there are some conditions under which the thalamus may not be reliable and here we need to exercise some caution. The problem with 'thin slicing' is while it can be a potential life saver, it also has the potential to lead us terribly astray. Your thalamus learns through your life experiences to distinguish between important sensory inputs requiring thought, sensory signals that are just 'noise' and sensory inputs that alert us to danger. It also makes judgments on the basis of what can be very flimsy evidence and that makes it prey to prejudice. What if your thalamus has learned that black men are more dangerous than white men? How would you even know this, since the thalamus operates before thought takes place? The fact is that we all have prejudices that we are not aware of. This is one very powerful reason for really good supervision that explores our practice in depth and is not just a box-ticking exercise. In Gladwell's book there is a fascinating account of a police shooting of Amadou Diallo in the Bronx which bears an uncanny similarity to the shooting of Charles de Menezes in Stockwell, London – in the panic, thin-slicing the wrong material led to an innocent man being killed. On a lighter note, he reports on the 'Warren Harding Error' – the error that well-spoken, tall, handsome, senatorial-looking men should make good Presidents of the United States. Warren Harding, however, 'was, most historians agree, one of the worst presidents in American history' (Gladwell 2005: 75).

There is another way in which your thalamus may mislead you. If you have a phobia, your thalamus is essentially labelling as dangerous inputs which are not dangerous. This is similar also to the way in which people who have PTSD may develop an overwhelming fear reaction to something that they associate with the traumatic event. So if, for example, you had been attacked and your head was repeatedly smashed against a red door, you might understandably get a sense of danger every time you see a red door even though red doors are no more a sign of danger than any other coloured door.

This exploration of how our brains and bodies work together is not to suggest that we operate solely by 'gut instinct' and intuition. Certainly these can alert us to the possibility of danger and the need to take a step back, but the real point is that there is a part of our brain that picks up when we are in trouble, seconds before our body reacts. If then we can learn to recognize that moment, it is suggested here that we may be able to programme ourselves to follow a predetermined protocol which will get us through the opening moments of the violence without our body becoming our enemy while at the same time avoiding any actions that might escalate the situation. This **survival schema** I call **front-end rapid reaction skills** to which we will return in Chapter 4.

Summary

In this chapter we have looked at how both our brain and body react and combine when under duress. We have also noted that the acute stress response – or the body's physical reaction to threat – is accompanied by parallel emergency psychological processes that help us to deal with fast-changing crises. It is suggested that it is not a reasonable, or always helpful goal to try to remain calm, but instead to know what you have to do to avoid entering into a state of panic. As violent behaviour often occurs faster than we are able to think, it is important that we understand the notion of rapid cognition and how we can make informed snap judgments based on reliable intuitions.

Top Tips
- Listen to your body – it may alert you to danger long before you are able to assess it formally.
- Notice that there are two kinds of warnings that come from the body – one is 'a sense' that things aren't right which should alert you to the need to slow things down and carry out a thorough risk assessment, while the other may come only seconds before the situation becomes dangerous.
- This second warning should trigger a prepared 'survival schema' – a protocol of front-end rapid reaction skills which will take you through the initial stages of the crisis without triggering a violent response and prevent your own body from shutting down or going into crisis.
- It is important not to battle with your body but to understand how it responds to imminent threat.

Chapter Three

Skills for Dealing with Difficult Reactive Aggression

Rising Tensions

In this chapter you will:

- learn about the processes underpinning difficult reaction aggression
- explore some of the key practice issues in working with people who are becoming increasingly agitated
- identify low level approaches for defusing agitated service users
- identify a specific skills for de-escalating behaviour that is approaching the pivotal point for reactive aggression

While at university I moved into a shared house with four friends. It was a good arrangement as we were following similar studies and got on well with one another. There was only one glitch – one of my housemates kept eating my cheese. Finally I decided to have it out with him. I'd rehearsed my speech well: 'Listen, I like cheese and you like cheese. We both like cheese and you could even say we are cheese lovers. The salient point here, however, is that it is my cheese. So please, in future, enjoy your own cheese and not mine.' I thought it was balanced, reasoned and respectful, so imagine my chagrin when he replied with, 'Woo woo! Chill out man, kids are dying in Biafra – get a perspective!' 'I have a perspective and that is that you need to keep your filthy mitts off my effing cheese!' I retorted. 'Hang loose mother goose!' came back the reply. By now I could feel my blood boil. I hate that feeling, but I turned away muttering to myself, 'Just walk away. If he wants to be a jerk let him be one. It's not worth it, you've dealt with the cheese issue Iain, now move on . . .'

And so I was resolved to do until the next day on my return from college I went to open the fridge. Sure enough my cheese was there – but with a huge tooth mark in it. From behind I heard someone enter the kitchen singing, 'On top of spaghetti, all covered in cheese.' I swung around to see him with a big smirk on his face. 'Howdy big cheese man!' Suddenly I found myself reaching for the kitchen knife and moving towards him, saying, 'Touch my cheese and you're a dead man!' I chased him up the stairs, down the stairs, into the garden and back through the house and onto the street. Even as I was doing this, I was also saying to myself, 'What are you doing Iain? Stop it, it's not worth it. Don't let him get to you – walk away!' Curiously, these very sensible thoughts had absolutely no effect – absurdly I was still chasing him around and about the house with a kitchen knife over a bit of cheese!

It's Not About the Cheese!

By now you might be wondering if it's wise to listen to a man who chases people around with knives over a bit of cheese – and of course I have to leave you to make your own decision about that! In my defence, that was the only time I recall having chased someone in anger. The point of the story, however, is that it was never really about the cheese. It was about feeling wronged and humiliated, abused and disrespected; it was about a sense of unfairness and a purposeful violation. If he had asked if he could have some of my cheese I would have willingly given it to him. If when confronted, had he simply said 'Sorry, I wasn't thinking' I would probably have replied, 'Don't worry about it.' Instead, however, he showed no grace only adding insult to injury.

The truth is that although superficially this was a potentially dangerous encounter, the chance of anything serious happening was close to zero. I would never have used the knife and my housemate knew that too. The whole thing was really more about communication and an illustration of what happens when communication fails. Undoubtedly this is the 'big story' when we consider escalating reactive aggression – which will undoubtedly be the most common form of aggression that helping professionals (and indeed people in general) will encounter. At one level this is a trivial example and rather ridiculous and yet at another a curious puzzle. How can a reasonably intelligent pair of young men, who actually get on quite well and who don't carry the burdens of the world on their shoulders, end up playing out such a pantomime – surely it was just a bit of larking about? But no, the blood was boiling, the emotions were high and all good sense was on holiday.

So let's look at this as a metaphor for escalating interactions between professionals and service users. The trigger was not the cheese but the breakdown in communication, the sense that my housemate really 'wasn't getting it'. At that point the situation could easily have been dealt with effectively as already suggested. As the communication continue to fail, I could feel the anger in me rising, yet still, as we will explore in this chapter, it would have been possible to defuse the situation. As the passions within me grew, a sense of injustice, of having been wronged took over. As my levels of arousal rose my ability to think clearly diminished to the point, the pivotal point, where I was no longer able to articulate what was going on for me. At that point my untutored limbic system took over and reason became a helpless onlooker. Notice that not only did reasoning play no useful part in this, but my friend's attempt to use reasoning simply poured oil on troubled waters. I was well aware that children were starving in Biafra and that my behaviour was becoming ridiculous – being told so really didn't help. Notice also that the 'issue', the cheese, was irrelevant – it could have been anything – but the sense of being wronged and the rising emotions as the communication failed were everything. Furthermore, it is worth noticing that skills my friend could have used early on in the interactions ('Sorry mate, I wasn't thinking') would not have been so nearly effective as the situation escalated. Clearly one size does not fit all.

Obviously service users are often operating under much greater duress (e.g. living in poverty, being in a violent or oppressive relationship, having mental health issues), often with fewer resources (e.g. not having English as their first language, having learning disabilities, poor physical health) and with much greater unwanted intrusions into their lives (e.g. child protection investigations, threats to their tenancies, bail conditions). With all these stressors in their lives it is quite understandable that sometimes they will react with aggression. My point, however, is that once that aggression begins to escalate it is the process, not the detail, that needs to be managed.

In professional practice there are two terms in common usage, often interchangeably, when we talk about reducing the tension and increasing safety. I am not aware that they have ever been differentiated or even recognized as different in the literature, but to me they represent different skill sets – and these are again distinct from the rapid reaction skills we will examine in Chapters 4 and 5. These terms are defusing skills and de-escalating skills. To me the former refer to those lower level skills used when dealing with a service user who is beginning to become upset, angry, irritated, frustrated or generally having a bad day. De-escalating skills however refer to those skills required when a service user is rapidly approaching the pivotal point, and the situation requires a much greater sense of urgency and precision (Figure 3.1). The difference is not only in what is boiling

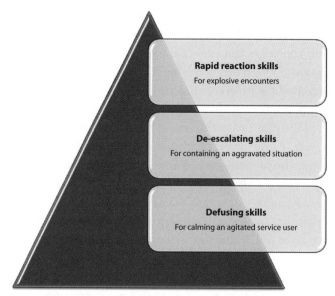

Figure 3.1. Skill Levels for Dealing with Reactive Aggression

up within the service user, but also in what resources, personal and professional, we can reasonably draw upon to deal with the burgeoning crisis.

Common Themes

Defusing, de-escalating and rapid reaction skills are all on the same behavioural trajectory and share a number of common themes. This is important because it means that if we develop our competence in one set of skills that will also put us on the right track to develop our competence in the other skill sets. Understanding these themes will also help guide our decision making when faced with aggression.

1 Do Something

It may sound like a statement of the obvious. After all if you see a customer waiting in the reception area clenching their fists, huffing and puffing, muttering oaths under their breath, going red and pacing up and down, would you really think that doing nothing would be an effective strategy? Their behaviour is going up, not down and the longer you take to intervene, the more difficult it will be. I imagine we can all agree that someone needs to do something even though we might hope it wasn't us. However, there are another two other schools of thought that suggest it is sometimes better to do nothing. One is the **cathartic approach** and the other is the **behavioural approach**.

The cathartic approach suggests that if a person is boiling up inside, it may be better to let them let off a little steam. In fairness, I used to believe this myself particularly when I was managing a therapeutic community for adolescents. Consider the following story:

> Joe is 16 years old and struts about the Unit as if he hasn't a care in the world. He tells you he has seen it all before, nothing fazes him, and he's got the T shirt. He wants you to think he is hard, mean and cool. He boasts about how many professionals he has 'got through' in his life, but actually all he really wants is to be left alone with his mum and dad. His mother has told him that if he really tries hard in the Unit, she would love to have him home for the Bank Holiday weekend. He won't admit it, but that means everything to him – and he makes sure he doesn't blow it this time. The day before his planned visit home his mother rings the staff to say that something has come up and unfortunately she won't be able to have Joe home for the weekend. They appeal to her, pointing out how hard Joe has been trying and how important it is to him, but she is resolute. Reluctantly, they go to tell Joe. 'Joe, your mum's just been on the phone and she says something has come up and so she can't have you home this weekend. She says she loves you, and would love to have you home another weekend, but unfortunately not this one. I am really sorry, Joe.' At this point Joe looks flushed and then starts saying, 'Why are you sorry? I'm not sorry, I didn't want to go anyway – so that's cool. They just sit in front of the TV all day long and do **** all – so if they're happy so am I.' Joe is clearly finding it hard to deal with the feelings that are welling up inside. The staff member repeats, 'I am really sorry Joe . . .' to which Joe screams '**** you!' and runs to his bedroom where he proceeds to trash the place. The staff member stays outside telling a colleague, 'Let him trash the room, how could his mother have done that to him?'

Clearly the worker was working on the implicit assumption that it was better for Joe to get it out of his system, the cathartic approach. So what do you imagine happened next? That Joe, having trashed the room then comes out feeling released, saying, 'I'm glad I got that one out of my system'? Not in a million years! Instead, as he trashed the room, he become more and more distressed, painting himself into a corner from which he could find no escape. Eventually his behaviour became so destructive that the staff had to physically restrain him for his own safety. Physically, emotionally and psychologically nothing was gained, but a lot was damaged and the question that was left was – why did they let it get so bad? Presumably because they thought Joe was getting it out of his system. Instead it would have been much better to have intervened a lot earlier, helping him to manage his escalating crisis. We are not sealed pneumatic plumbing systems. Just because we express anger does not mean we get rid of it. Indeed the research, if anything, suggests the exact opposite. Geen and Quanty (1977), reviewing a considerable body of evidence, concluded that 'the theory of catharsis is empirically false', while Bushman et al. (1999) characterize the catharsis theory as 'largely discredited' and 'incorrect'. The error is in confusing an idea intended as a therapeutic tool with a crisis management technique. Therapy is slow and long yet crises are fast and short – they exist on opposite ends of a spectrum.

The other 'do nothing' theory comes from the behavioural notion that you shouldn't reinforce bad behaviour. Indeed if you take a child to see a behavioural therapist because they have been 'acting out', it is quite likely that the prescription will be along the lines of encouraging you not to reinforce the bad behaviour, but to focus on the positives. That's fair enough and in the long term that might show some real dividends, but in the short term the behaviour is likely to be much worse as the child tries with increasing desperation to get their 'behaving badly' strategy back on track. Once again, when we talk about facing danger, we are talking about effecting immediate behaviour change, not long-term therapeutic gains.

Indeed, if, going back to my earlier contention, most reactive aggression stems from a breakdown in communication, then refusing to communicate clearly makes no sense at all. Imagine that you are upset with your partner and you just want to let them know how upset you are. How would you feel if they steadfastly ignored you – or perhaps worse just said 'talk to the hand'?

> **Practice point** Dealing with aggression is about good, but very simple communication.

2 Less is Better

This is the corollary to the point above and in many ways the mantra that echoes throughout this book. Crises demand action from us, but often that action goes well beyond the point of effectiveness. This book is about professional practice and to my mind, good professional practice is often about keeping things very simple. Aggression, however, stirs passions within us and aggressors can be quite skilled at pressing our buttons. The problem is that if we don't know what to do we are likely to do nothing at all, or far too much. I probably face danger far less than many of you. I do, however, watch a fair amount of dangerous behaviour at a safe distance – usually incidents caught on CCTV in hospitals, police stations, prisons, residential homes, reception areas and public places – and while I haven't conducted a systematic review of these observations, my impressions are clear and consistent. Staff who are effective and competent in crises tend to intervene early and keep it simple. Staff who tend to get into bother generally don't intervene early enough, and when they do, they complicate matters. Sometimes they have effectively managed the crisis, but then have to have the last word, refuse to let it go, want to win, be clever, or showboat. Obviously, if we don't know what to do, it is likely that we will do more rather than less because we don't know when we have done what we need to do! Hopefully this chapter will go some way to addressing that need.

> **Practice point** Keep things very simple and focus on resolving the crisis rather than winning the argument.

3 Sensing and Going Under the Radar

Just like my cheese story these are not moments of reason, but moments to get to the point of reason. We are professionals and hopefully our default position is to facilitate fruitful and respectful communication, effective problem solving and excellent service delivery. That, however, skips a couple of steps at least. For us to achieve that goal, both we and the service user must be able to communicate at that level. The impediments can be transitory (e.g. they may be raging and we may be fearful) or constant (e.g. they may have a learning disability and we might be hard of hearing). Either way, if we predicate our approach on the ability to reason in a crisis, we have already lost our way. Reasoning is for later, as are the loftier ideals of therapeutic practice. These are fast-moving heated moments and just as the service user may lose the capacity to think clearly, so might we. A kinder approach for us and them would to be to avoid this poisoned fruit.

Like our service users, we too have fears, stresses and anxieties. Sometimes service users assume we have received an inoculation against fear, or more likely, they are just much more focussed on their own crisis and not ours. Think back to my cheese story. Two bright, (well, I know he was) young people who liked each other waged a temporary and potentially violent war because they couldn't think their way through an emotional problem. Formal logic played no major part. But there is another way. We are sentient beings. We don't just think things, we feel them and sense them. Now to the scientists among us this might feel like woolly territory, yet nonetheless, I would argue that the majority of significant interactions between professionals and service users are not thought about but sensed. The goal is not to get the service user to understand, but to sense. To sense that you are listening, that you are on their side, that it is easier to follow you than go against you, that there will be no loss of face, that their problems are lessening, and that the demands on them are decreasing.

Now before we go any further, I'd like to take this opportunity to introduce another concept that will infiltrate our discussions from here on in. It is a simple idea based on the premise that people cannot resist or react against forces that they are not aware of. This is, in some ways, the skill of the hypnotist or magician. The converse of this is that people can very easily resist or react against forces that they are aware of – and the easiest forces to resist are those that involve reason. Reason simply invites argument in a crisis. So 'under the radar skills' are those that affect the aggressor's behaviour without their awareness.

Consider the following:

> A GP is visiting a family home where there is a sick child. As they attend to the child an acrimonious row breaks out between the mother and father. The GP turns to the parents and says, 'Please calm down, the pair of you. You are upsetting your daughter.' At this point the father becomes further enraged screaming, 'Who the hell do you think you are, coming into our house, poking your nose into our business?!' The GP replies, 'I am just concerned for the welfare of your daughter.' To which the father starts moving menacingly towards the GP saying, 'And you think we don't? Is that it?'

Superficially everything the GP said was perfectly reasonable but the effect was to further enrage the situation. This, in effect, is a much more subtle version of my cheese story. The GP tried reason to solve an emotional and behavioural problem and in so doing poured oil on troubled waters inviting a potentially dangerous argument. The GP's motives were honourable but their overt intervention merely invited resistance and hostility. Our task is to identify ways, possibly under the radar, of intervening that do not invite an escalation.

Practice point Non-verbal communications that are 'sensed' are much more difficult to reject than attempts to reason with the aggressor.

4 Containment Not Resolution

This is a corollary to the 'do something, not more, less but always something' edict. De-escalating and defusing skills are not about resolving the crisis that triggered the aggression. They are simply designed to minimize the risk of a situation becoming more dangerous, or to take the heat out of an already explosive situation. Nonetheless, it is very easy to fall into the trap of trying to solve the problem too soon. Often people will respond to escalating reactive aggression with questions – 'What's happened?' 'What do you want from me?' 'Why are you behaving like this?' 'How can I help?' These are obviously very reasonable enquiries and under normal circumstances may be quite helpful and appropriate – but here we are not talking about normal circumstances. By asking questions we are placing demands upon the aggressor not only to understand their own behaviour but to articulate it in a way that does not embarrass them. This is a complex job requiring sophisticated insights and refined interpersonal skills. If you think back to my cheese story, I would have had a hard job finding a dignified way of explaining my behaviour if asked. As we saw earlier with the Yerkes-Dodson Law, beyond a certain level of arousal performance at complex tasks deteriorates significantly, and so by asking questions we might effectively increase the service user's stress levels. Questions are for later when the levels of arousal have reduced and the immediate danger has passed. An important principle in a crisis is to do just one thing at a time and not to move on from that one thing until it has been achieved.

Practice point The task is to establish safety and not to resolve the problem. The problem can be addressed later.

5 Fear is Your Friend

Many professionals believe that it is important not to show fear as this will give power to the aggressor. There may be some truth in that, in some circumstances, but I would argue that there is not enough truth in it to make it your creed. Fear is perfectly healthy and appropriate, it is what tells us to wake up and be alert, to take care and to get ready for action. If we didn't feel fear, our thalamic radar (see Chapter 2) would be broken and we would find ourselves blundering into all kinds of calamitous situations. I have come across many people, service users, professionals and personal acquaintances, who have proudly proclaimed to me that they don't feel fear. What I think they are saying is something quite different – that fear doesn't make them panic. Similarly, just about every book I have read about dealing with aggression has highlighted the importance of remaining calm when in truth the important thing is not necessarily to stay calm – which may not be achievable or even helpful – but not to panic.

We should not avoid fear, but try to make fear our friend rather than our master. It is to be embraced and channelled. In a crisis we have enough to struggle with, without having to struggle with ourselves as well. This is why in Chapter 2 we looked at how our brain and body work in a crisis, because trying to work against yourself is a thankless task.

> **Practice point** Rather than trying not to show fear, it is much better to get on with what has to be done. Panic is to be avoided and this occurs when we don't know what to do. So even if the defusing and de-escalating skills identified in this chapter contain no magic, the fact that you have got something to do will keep your bodily reactions in check.

6 The Dysphoric Crisis

As the aggressor's level of arousal increases, as they get pumped up or wound up, their capacity to listen, think, problem-solve and articulate diminish and at the same time strategies that rely on these faculties become increasingly ineffective. The pivotal point for escalating reactive aggression is the point at which the demands upon them exceed their immediate resources to cope with those demands. At this point they will experience intense stress and pressure, seconds may feel like an eternity and the embarrassment of not knowing how to respond may be overwhelming. They are, in effect, in a psychological vacuum and the only way to survive is to fill it. Suddenly the limbic system takes over in a wholly untutored way and they begin to act out violently. The function of the violence, however, is simply to buy time, even just the next second perhaps in the hope that they will rediscover their way through the crisis, and to deflect from the humiliation of not knowing what to do. Defusing skills are to lessen the tension and prevent the vacuum opening up. De-escalating skills are to fill the vacuum as it opens up. Rapid skills are for when the vacuum is already being filled by the aggressor.

Practice point The pivotal point occurs when the crisis is in the balance and very small changes in the driving and restraining forces can lead to large behaviour changes – for better or worse.

7 Personalizing and Depersonalizing

Is it better for the aggressor to see us as a person or as a professional? The answer to this question will undoubtedly inform how we deal with the aggressor and as usual the answer is not a simple yes or no. Clearly, if the aggressor is wanting you to do your job, then they probably don't really care about you as a person but as a means to an end. A great deal of the aggression towards us as professionals has very little to do with us personally – they are angry with the system, with authority, with their situation – it's just that we happen to represent all those things right now. The general advice (Davies and Frude 2000; Linsley 2006) is that we should depersonalize the issue and personalize ourselves which makes good sense. If you are a housing officer about to serve a court order for the eviction of a tenant, or a social worker about to remove a child from their parents, or a residential worker enforcing a rule you are acting not through personal choice or preference, but on behalf of the courts or your employer. It's true that you may feel a sense of responsibility as you are the one involved in the process and to the service user you are the face of the system that is imposing sanctions upon them. At such times it clearly makes sense to follow the advice of Davies and Frude (2000: module 13, p. 13) and be ruthless with the issue but gracious with people; that is 'handle the person with the dignity and respect that all deserve, while at the same time being clear that the task in hand has to be completed'.

So far so good. However, it is undoubtedly the case that the most common form of violence is domestic violence and as this occurs in a highly personal relationship it might suggest that personalizing oneself could put you in greater danger. Personally I would find it more frightening if I thought a service user had it in for me personally than if I just happened to be the unlucky face of the system. Confusing? Well here we need to be clear about the difference between the long story and the short story; between the ongoing situation and the incident. Domestic violence is the long story. Two people are in an intimate relationship over a period of time and during that period violence periodically erupts. A threatening and oppressive atmosphere may be ever present, and as we will see in Chapter 7, that may feel worse than the violence itself. Nonetheless, the violence isn't there most of the time, and it goes without saying that the longer two people spend in one another's company the more likely over that period things will happen. Indeed, it is likely that most abusive relationships started off as good relationships, so maybe rather than just equating personal relationships with violence we should look a little closer at the short story – what happens between two people when hostilities break out.

It is clearly much easier to attack an object that another human being – that's why we kick a chair or punch the wall. Racists do not view their targets in personal terms, but as 'one of them', faceless, all the same. The fact that they depersonalize their targets makes the attack all the more likely. Military violence is also depersonalized. Soldiers are not necessarily intrinsically more violent than anyone else but their training, their drills and their orders allow acts of violence to be depersonalized – it's the war, they are the enemy, it's orders, a mission, a target or a hit. Not only can we depersonalize the person or people that we are in conflict with, but we can depersonalize ourselves. Zimbardo and his colleagues (Haney et al. 1973) powerfully demonstrated in the Stanford Prison experiment how the processes of de-individuation (loss of one's own individual sense of self) and depersonalization of others could temporarily but dramatically lead a group of psychologically healthy, normal college students to become cruel, vindictive and abusive. Likewise, football fans can swear at, jeer, taunt and attempt to intimidate the opposition fans during the match while in the crowd, and yet have a good humoured laugh about it with the same people at work. Playing violent computer games is another example demonstrating how depersonalizing the target and losing a sense of one's own individuality can facilitate violent behaviour.

So, why is it then that violence occurs so often in intimate partner relationships? Clearly there are many reasons: these are emotionally charged relationships, both partners share the same living space and arrangements over an extended period of time, one or both may feel trapped and see no way out, alcohol may play an important factor, and so on. Actually, when the relationship is personalized it can be very safe. One partner might say to the other that they would never harm a hair on their body, that they would do anything for the partner, nothing would be too much. Yet when the scales fall off their eyes, frustrations and resentments creep in and as their irritability rises, what do they do? They start calling their partner names and in so doing are depersonalizing them and this may be the prelude that makes the attack all the more likely.

One more example. It is quite conceivable that an angry service user might not like me, or for that matter, you. They might not like our sense of humour, our dress sense, our accent, our approach to the work, or the decisions that we make. They get on fine with the rest of our team – it is specifically us that they take a strong dislike to. I think we would have to accept that this is not a case of being angry with the system, but specifically with us – and it's personal. Let's call this situation A.

On the other hand there will be probably more occasions where they are not specifically angry with us, but because we just happen to be there, or that we represent the system, authority, because we remind them of the mother or father, or because they think we are not like them. In this case they are not angry with us personally – if we weren't there someone else would be the target of the wrath. We will call this situation B. Which situation would be more dangerous for us, A or B?

For many of us, situation A would feel more uncomfortable because it implies that we may not be as perfect as we would like to think, but that is not the same as being more dangerous. Although they may see us as flawed human beings, it is hard to believe that they would want to kill us for that. However, if they don't see us as a human being, but just part of some faceless bureaucratic machine it would be possible to project all the ills of their world on us. The skill, therefore, is to present ourselves as three-dimensional human beings who are doing their best to do a difficult but non-negotiable job with another distressed human being.

> **Practice point** Depersonalize the issue but do not allow yourself to be depersonalized.

8 Mood-matching

Breakwell (1997), Davies and Frude (2000) and Linsley (2006) all refer to the concept or practice of **mood-matching** as an effective interpersonal strategy in communicating with an aggressive person. In some ways the phrase is unfortunate because it suggests that the professional should match or mirror the mood of the aggressor, and given that mood may well be hostile I think that we can all see that that may not result in a happy outcome. The idea is that if we are talking to someone who is depressed, we might slow down ourselves and speak in a lower tone. Similarly, if we are talking to someone who is happy or excitable we too might become a bit more upbeat. Conversely, if we try to cheer up a depressed individual by becoming chirpy and upbeat, they are likely to brush us off and tell us to leave them alone. At the same time if a service user is shouting at us, talking in a slow, calm, quiet manner may not actually be experienced as calming at all. They may not even notice you, or if they do they might feel that you just don't get it.

Mood-matching doesn't mean that we should match the mood of the service user. If you were struggling with depression would you really want to see a counsellor who was just as depressed as you? No, you would want to feel that the counsellor can empathize with you but also provide a ray of hope. Clearly, it is not helpful to become angry with an angry service user. Mood-matching involves *not* copying the aggressor's behaviour, or indeed matching their mood, but intervening at a similar level of intensity, but with concern. This may involve raising our voice to the same level as that of the service user but not to match their mood (angry) or mirror their behaviour (aggressive).

> **Practice point** To make the communication effective, you should not match the mood of the aggressor but you will probably have to match the intensity – with concern and a desire to resolve the problem.

9 Non-verbal Communications

Braithwaite (2001: 76–87) emphasizes the importance of non-verbal communications in dealing with an aggressor, identifying 14 common forms that this can take. Important as these are, however, they are incredibly sophisticated communications and very slight alterations in posture, gaze, movement, facial muscles, etc. can completely change their meaning. These communications are so deep and subtle, in fact, that no number of words will ever adequately describe them. Often on training courses I am asked if it is right to return the gaze of an aggressor or avert it and of course this is a very sensible enquiry. On the one hand some people believe that good eye contact is necessary to show that you are paying attention, to read the situation and to show that you are still in control at least of yourself. Others believe that direct eye contact could be confrontational, provoke the aggressor and frightening for the staff member – and that it is better not to get into an eye-balling contest. The trouble here, is that eye contact is being discussed as if it were just one thing.

> Take a look at the photos of the eyes in Figure 3.2. Look directly at each one in turn for about ten seconds and imagine being confronted by this man. What do you think returning his gaze would mean in each case? How do you think it would affect you and what effect do you think it would have on him? Is it the same or different in each case? Now look at the pictures again and imagine that the eyes are connected to the corresponding pictures of the lower part of the face. Does that change anything?

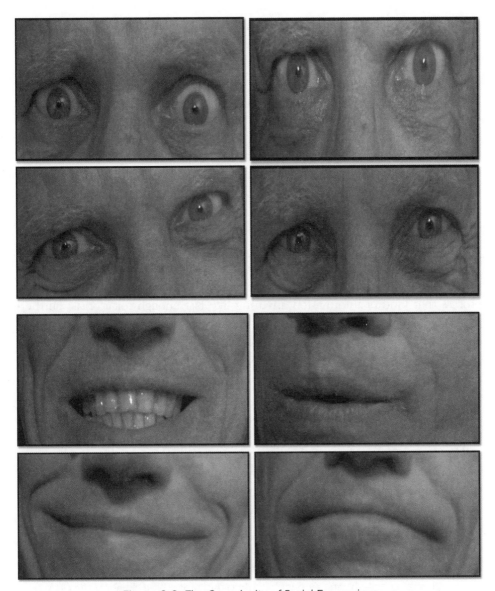

Figure 3.2. The Complexity of Facial Expressions

Clearly the eyes communicate a great deal but equally clearly not all eye contact is the same. Slight changes in the muscles around the eyes can change the meaning enormously as can the ratio between the pupil, the iris and the surrounding white sclera. Furthermore, in some ways the eyes by themselves can be misleading as the total meaning can only be understood once the rest of the face is taken into consideration.

Now consider that eye contact is not a one way process, but a two way process that reverberates between you and the person that you are looking at. Do you feel the same making eye contact with a person that you know well as opposed to a stranger? Does this change according to how confident you are feeling, or if the person you are looking at is older, younger, taller, shorter or if you are attracted to them or not? Now let's assume that you have got all this worked out, what about the cultural variations? In British culture not to look someone in the eye can appear shifty, while in Nigeria and East Asia it is respectful not to look at the dominant person in the eye (Galanti 2004). Mind-boggling isn't it? And so far we have only begun to scratch the surface of only one of Braithwaite's (2001) 14 aspects of body language that are important in dealing with an aggressor! Clearly there is far too much going on for us to stand any chance of micro-managing these communications.

The non-verbal signals that go between people in conflict are clearly sophisticated and critical but they cannot be prescribed, and our frontal cortex cannot process that kind of information anything like fast enough for a crisis. Furthermore, trying to behave according to such crude body language diktats increases our chances of getting it wrong, places unnecessary pressure upon us and is very likely to send out confusing signals to the aggressor. Indeed by definition it is almost impossible to adequately describe our non-verbal communications verbally and yet most of us, unless we are autistic, can usually read other people's body language instantly. So, during a crisis or confrontation, I suggest we don't think about our non-verbal behaviour and my experience is that as long as we know what to do, and have a genuine wish to resolve the crisis, that will take care of itself. Of course, we should all strive to become more self-aware, seeking feedback from others about how we come across and how we might communicate with others more effectively – but that form of learning should be taking place every day, not in a crisis.

> **Practice point** Do not try to micro-manage your non-verbal behaviour. If your attitude is right – having a concern to help and resolve the situation – your non-verbal behaviour will manage itself.

10 Boundaries

We have boundaries set out by our professional codes of conduct and by our employers through policies, procedures and our job descriptions. These are pretty much non-negotiable – if you are a doctor and notice some unexplained injuries on a child, it doesn't matter how much the child or their parents plead, you have to report your findings. As indicated earlier, however, you don't have to be mean, blaming or vindictive about this; you can be gracious but, nonetheless resolute. However, our work cannot be done by computers or robots because we work with people who are dynamic, multilayered, multi-faceted, fascinating and complex – and in working with those people we have to draw heavily upon our own humanity. Our tools and resources are ourselves and in the process these can lose their edge (professional burnout) or become damaged (trauma) – both of which we will return to later. Our responsibility to ourselves and our employer's responsibility to us is to maintain our resourcefulness and mental health. Our job is not to be abused or denigrated, but to provide some form of professional service. Being abused or put down are not part of the job, but hazards that go along with doing the job – and hazards need to be actively managed. Laptops and data projectors have electrical cables, but trainers don't just leave cables lying around on the floor because they go with the territory. They find a way of managing the risk. In the same way, we should not accept abuse because it is good neither for us nor for the perpetrator. Now while this chapter and many of those that follow are about what we have to do 'right now' in the face of dangerous behaviour, the truth is that for many of us, what happens right now might also set the scene for what follows in the future. If you are a residential worker and a resident is abusive to you and this is not actively managed at the time, they may become even more abusive the next time, and indeed other residents might take this as a signal that this is the way to go. Here, I am not talking about what sanctions might be applied by your manager when the abuse is reported, but how you can effectively manage your personal boundaries in the face of someone who is being abusive. This is an essential survival skill that runs through all aspects of our professional practice but one which is rarely addressed or articulated. More on this in the next section.

> **Practice point** Being abused is not a part of the job, but a hazard that goes along with it and hazards need to be managed.

Defusing Skills

These are the 'low arousal skills' most associated with professional practice and are those most expected by the general public of professional behaviour. In general that is not so difficult to define – I expect a professional to be socially skilled, respectful, pleasant, understanding, knowledgeable, reliable and trustworthy, to be able to listen to me, be competent and helpful. I expect the same of myself and I would hope that those that judge me would do so also. We are also human beings, not angels, and we have faults and failings. Things are happening in our own lives as well as in the lives of our service users and sometimes it's not the really big things that get under our skin but the little things against which we are much less defended. Sometimes words can hurt more than sticks and stones and it can help not only to know that we should respond professionally but how to do so.

Here we are talking about dealing with situations where someone is beginning to express discontent that will clearly rise if not addressed – and sooner rather than later. The situation is certainly becoming more uncomfortable, but it is still some way off the pivotal point and the feeling would be that as long as the situation can be dealt with appropriately a crisis can be avoided. This may not even involve a service user – it could be a colleague in a meeting who starts venting their frustration at recent cutbacks, or a course participant on a training course who is annoyed at having to attend against their wishes. These are uncomfortable, but not necessarily uncommon situations. The situation doesn't feel explosive or dangerous right now, but there may be a fear that unless this is handled well, it could get worse.

The first point I would like to make is that our own levels of anxiety will be far greater if we don't know what to do. In that sense knowing what to do, even if our recipe doesn't hold any magical ingredients, at least helps us to feel more confident and provides us with some direction. Also if the complainant senses that you know what you are doing they may let you get on with it as that takes the pressure off them. So being competent is the best way to manage our own fears and anxieties.

It seems to me that defusing skills draw upon ideas from different, but often overlapping sources:

- customer care approaches: treating the complainant with dignity and respect; recognizing that they may have a valid complaint; conveying that they have a right to expect a service; showing a commitment to resolving their complaint;
- assertiveness: the ability to respond in a non-aggressive, respectful manner while also being able to make reasonable demands of the aggressor; the ability to keep things simple and to keep the focus on behaviour;
- listening and problem-solving skills: the ability to make the aggressor feel that they are being listened to and taken seriously;
- things not to do: like wagging your finger, rolling your eyes, or telling the complainant to 'calm down!'.

At this level, as professional helpers we can exercise considerable discretion and choice in the way we go about defusing the situation because the situation is not yet critical and there is a margin for error. That is, if our approach appears ineffective or is worsening the situation, we can try something else. Furthermore, while I hope that these aren't everyday situations, they can be quite common and this means that we can practise and develop these skills. The same cannot be said of the rapid reaction skills that we will examine in Chapter 5. However, it strikes me that the better we are at these low arousal defusing skills, the better we will be prepared to deal with the more dangerous behaviour. This is because defusing, de-escalating and rapid reaction skills all follow a similar behavioural trajectory and the skills are not so vastly different per se; the major differences lie in the precision and intensity with which they need to be applied, and on the extent to which we have to manage our own emotional, physiological and psychological reactions to the crisis. So there are two great advantages in refining our defusing skills: first, in many cases intervening at this level will prevent the behaviour from escalating to the point where other skills are needed; and second, in becoming more comfortable and competent with the skills at this level we are effectively becoming more attuned to a style of intervening that will be increasingly necessary as the danger increases.

Consider the following scenario:

> A patient, Mr Johnson, arrives at reception in the medical centre where you work. For whatever reason he is clearly unhappy and letting the receptionist and everyone else in the waiting area know it. The receptionist's best attempts to deal with his complaint are having little effect. Other patients are being kept waiting and they are becoming increasingly agitated. You are called to deal with Mr Johnson . . .

We might be torn between competing agendas. I might feel annoyed that Mr Johnson has given the receptionist such a tough time and upset the other patients. I could walk into the reception area saying 'Sir, I understand that you have a complaint and we will deal with that, but you have upset the receptionist and the other patients and that is not acceptable.' In fact, if I'm honest, I am sure I have said almost exactly that in situations in the past – maybe with the idea of offering support to the receptionist and other patients while setting the standard for acceptable behaviour. Unfortunately, if my goal is to defuse the situation it fails miserably in as much as it leaves Mr Johnson feeling publicly humiliated when he was already feeling aggrieved. Our objectives would be to calm the situation, resolve Mr Johnson's complaint, reassure the receptionist and the patients and send a clear signal about acceptable behaviour within the medical centre – but not all at the same time! So let's look again.

1 Prepare

We won't always have this luxury, but when we do we should use it. Make sure that you know the patient's name at least. It makes a big difference starting out with their name rather than the somewhat anonymous and officious sir or madam. It also makes sense to have prepared how you will introduce yourself to Mr Johnson. It may also be worth taking the time to ensure that you can greet Mr Johnson in good spirits and not as if you are irritated by this unsolicited interruption into your week by schedule.

2 Engage and Isolate

You approach Mr Johnson in a friendly but businesslike manner saying something along the lines of:

'Hello Mr Johnson, I am (your name and position). Perhaps you would like to come with me and we can go over what has happened.'

It is advisable not to use words or phrases like upset, angry, annoyed, problem, concern or issue at this point, especially in front of an audience, as Mr Johnson may take that as a cue to continue with his complaint in the reception area. By removing him from the audience you are also providing him with a face-saving way of backing down.

3 Slow Down

Here I am not suggesting that we keep Mr Johnson waiting, which could be his original complaint, but reduce the pace of the interactions before attempting to deal with his complaint. For example:

- offer him a seat;
- check that he is comfortable;
- ask if he'd like a drink of tea, coffee or water;
- tell him you need to get a pen and paper to take notes.

Just small delays may be sufficient bring his level of arousal down.

4 Attend

Once both of you are settled, invite Mr Johnson to tell you what has happened. Do not introduce words like angry, upset, problem, etc. unless he has explicitly used those words already. Simply,

> 'Mr Johnson, tell me what has happened. Start at the beginning and don't feel you have to rush.'

Then just listen, actively, showing that you are following what he is saying – nod, smile, repeat key phrases, paraphrase, ask for more detail. If he looks like speeding up, slow him down by asking him to go back over something he said earlier. Whatever you do, do not disagree, contradict, challenge, or put forward your own view or that of the service. Even if Mr Johnson tells you things that you know are palpably not true – 'I was promised, that under the new NHS funding arrangements if I couldn't get my ingrown toe nail seen to within a month locally I would be entitled to travel to California for the operation – and it hasn't happened!' – do not challenge. At most you might try

> 'So, Mr Johnson, what you are saying is that you were led to believe that you had an entitlement to travel to California on the NHS and this hasn't happened and that is what has upset you?'

If he agrees you might sympathize.

> 'Well Mr Johnson, I guess if somehow my hopes had been raised and then dashed, I'd be upset too. Can you tell me how this came about?'

You are not agreeing or disagreeing, simply allowing him to have his say and to be taken seriously. This may be facilitated by asking him if it's okay for you to take some notes. Once he has had his say, you can demonstrate that you have been listening by offering him back a summary of what he has said. If at any point Mr Johnson's behaviour becomes unacceptable simply say

'Mr Johnson, I am trying to help you, so I would appreciate it if you (wouldn't swear/would remain seated/lower your voice, etc.).'

5 Problem-solve

Once he feels he has had his say and you have checked that he agrees with your understanding of the situation you may wish to ask him what he would like to happen next. It may well be that he doesn't feel he has to take it any further. If he does, clarify what that is, and if it's not possible be honest but then look at what might be possible. If you have to refer him on to see someone else it might be helpful to try to do that while he is there.

6 Review

Finally check that he feels satisfied that the issue has been dealt with. It may also be worth exploring how he might be able to address any future concerns without upsetting the receptionist or the patients in the waiting area.

Most situations can probably be handled quite effectively at this 'good customer care' level. In some cases, however, the service user may be already too wound up to engage in this defusing process, at least initially, and that is where de-escalation skills come in.

De-escalation Skills

Consider the following:

During a group session, Paul, who has been looking tense throughout, suddenly interrupts you in mid-sentence: 'I've had enough of this. This is a load of *******! We're not getting anywhere and I can't take much more of this ****!' He begins to get out of his chair . . .

Now although this may not be the most dramatic of situations, and I'm sure most of us have encountered much worse, it looks like it might turn out not to be one of your better days at the office. Understandably we might feel a sense of responsibility, a feeling that we are being criticized, maybe some embarrassment and we need to respond appropriately. As I have already said, the pressure might feel a lot less if we already know how we will respond.

Essentially at this level if the service user can 'sense' that they do not have to battle against the system, that their complaint or issue will be heard and dealt with efficiently, that they are being treated respectfully and that it is easier to work with us than against us – then most situations will not escalate any further.

1 Slow Down and Focus

The first thing is to intervene quickly. This is not just to stem the torrent from Paul, but because if we don't other group members might step in. However, in intervening we always have to bear in mind the mantra 'don't do more, do less but do something'. We could say, 'Paul, there's no reason to behave like that'. However, that would be more rather than less, and he may well come back with 'I'll behave how I bloody well like!' or 'Who the hell do you think you are to tell me how to behave?' or 'Screw you!' – the list is endless. Our quick intervention has in fact escalated rather than de-escalated the situation. Instead a more effective front-end intervention would have been to simply use and repeat his name and no more until Paul slows down and looks at us. How we do this depends on too many factors to prescribe – one's personal style, the relationship we have with Paul, how upset Paul is and so forth – however, the important thing is that we do this in a concerned and congruent way. That is the tone of our voice, eye contact and body movements should convey that we are taking him seriously, that right now he is the sole focus of our attention and that we wish to minimize his distress. Exactly how you and I might do that is likely to be different because we are different people and we affect people in different ways. It may be necessary to raise our voices if only to gain his attention and the way we use our voice should convey a desire to communicate. At this level, it really doesn't matter too much if we are talking to a child, a person with learning disabilities, an older person with confusion, or whoever. We are simply trying to make safe contact with them in the simplest and most basic ways.

By restricting our initial interventions to their name, or in situations where you don't have their name, sir or madam, we achieve several important things:

- We are focussing their attention on us and although we might not be too keen on that, the truth is that we cannot de-escalate or defuse their behaviour if they are not focussed and paying attention to us.
- We are slowing them down – when I was running around the house with the kitchen knife if someone had slowed me down, maybe I could have listened to myself and walked away.
- By interjecting repeatedly with their name (or similar) we would also be interrupting their flow of angry thoughts and potentially creating a 'safe opening' into which we might intervene.

- We are also signalling to Paul that we are not going to complicate the situation or increase the demands on him, for example, by asking questions or requiring him to justify the behaviour.
- We are letting other group members know that we are dealing with this.

This 'slowing' and 'attention-grabbing' process should result in Paul focussing on us without providing any ammunition that he might throw back at us. At the same time it doesn't place any extra demands upon him. As he finds it increasingly difficult to think about what he is trying to communicate he is likely to put the onus back on us, 'Yeah, what?' or maybe 'Will you just shut up?' Either way we have created a (psychological) space into which we can now safely enter. If they tell us to shut up we can appear to give them what they want. 'Okay Paul, I'll shut up but . . .' or if they say 'Yeah, what?' we can move on to the next step, which is to engage with them directly.

2 Engage

There are various criteria we have to meet if we are to be able to safely and successfully engage with Paul at this level. This is the pre-verbal level and although we may use words, it is not the words that are critical, but what Paul senses. For him to allow you in he has to sense that you have 'got the message'. It is not enough, however, if he thinks you have received the formal message, i.e. that he does not consider this group to be a good use of his time – but the emotional message too – which is essentially that he is not very happy and he really needs you to know this! Furthermore he is only likely to allow you to engage with him if he senses that:

- it will be easier for him rather than more difficult;
- you want to help;
- this will involve no loss of dignity or embarrassment.

So 'the script' runs something along the lines of:

> 'Paul, I can see that you are (upset, angry, unhappy), and I'd really like to (help you, answer your question, sort this out).'

This lets him know that you have received the emotional message and that you are trying to respond helpfully.

3 Offer Assistance

Once this has been achieved and not before, we are ready to take the engagement further. We need to have his attention, slow him down, acknowledge his emotional state, let him know that we are committed to resolving the immediate and current situation. However, we also need to place some boundaries around his behaviour and also let him know that we have some boundaries of our own. The first part of this is guiding his behaviour back towards a more reasonable and acceptable level. The focus here has to be on behaviour and not what might be his problem. Some aspect of his behaviour will be contributing to the problem or getting in the way of its resolution. It's not generally very difficult to spot, but we may have a tendency to voice it in ways that are not helpful: 'calm yourself', 'there's no need for that', 'please don't be so disrespectful', 'behave yourself', 'don't be so silly', 'stop messing about', 'you're being ridiculous now'. These, however, are escalating not de-escalating statements, examples of doing more rather than less, and are likely to inflame rather than defuse. Indeed they are extremely unclear statements that provide very little direction for the aggressor. Instead, following the offer of assistance, a single action behavioural demand is more effective – and the focus of that demand should be on whatever they are doing, right now, that is getting in the way of you providing that help. So if he is standing over you and crowding you out, you say:

> 'I'd really like to help you Paul, but I need you to step back and give me some space.' If he is shouting: 'Paul, I'd really like to help you, but you need to stop shouting.'

If he is waving his fist at you say:

> 'Paul, we're going to sort this out, but stop waving your fist at me.'

Again the tone and volume of your voice, your facial expression, eye contact and body language will make a big difference, but it is a thankless task to focus on these micro-behaviours while the confrontation is taking place. More important is your attitude and that will direct these micro-behaviours automatically without you needing to think about them. You may have to engage with some intensity, but you are not matching their mood – meeting anger with anger – but with concern and a genuine will to resolve the situation.

Clearly it would be wonderful if it was always so simple. Paul may well be running hot and not able to respond immediately, or he may not trust that you know how to deal with the situation, or find it difficult to back down in front of his peers. He may well come back with statements like 'Why should I?' or 'Who are you to tell me what to do?' or worse, or indeed he might carry on by simply ignoring you. Here it is important not to complicate the situation, to negotiate and certainly not to threaten. The simplest, safest and probably most effective strategy here is to use the **broken record technique**. It is an example of 'not doing more, doing less, but doing something'. This is a technique often suggested in assertiveness training courses and involves acting a bit like an old vinyl record that has got stuck in the groove and keeps repeating the same part of the track. So if you don't get the desired response from Paul, don't vary the message, or add to it, simply repeat the message again and again. So if you said, 'Paul, I'd like to help you, but you need to stop shouting' and he continues shouting you simply repeat 'Please stop shouting' and no more. Certainly not even 'Please stop shouting, or…' which is an example of doing more rather than less and may offer the ammunition to be used against you – 'Or what?!' There are some caveats here, however. The term 'broken record' implies a certain amount of monotony and that is NOT what we are after – we are not trying to bore them into submission! That would be counter-productive. Imagine trying to convey to someone how upset you are only to see them chewing gum and rolling their eyes to the ceiling – it would be pretty much the same thing. No, we don't repeat in a monotonous or disinterested way but in a way that conveys that:

- we urgently want to resolve the situation;
- they have our undivided attention;
- we will keep it simple and that we will not be buffeted by their behaviour;
- we will treat them with respect.

This involves using the 'broken record' technique in an animated and expressive manner. It is not necessarily the words that matter, but the communication that takes place under the radar. Other reasons for keeping verbal language to a minimum include the fact that for some service users English may not be their first language and so be confusing. If they are really upset they may not be able to understand what you are saying, and this may be further complicated if the service user has hearing loss, is aphasic, has learning disabilities, or just has a very argumentative temperament. Another caveat is, of course, that the application of any technique does not mean that commonsense should take a holiday. If the aggressor is pointing a gun at you and after asking them to put it down several times they say, 'You say that one more time and I'll blow your head off!' you should listen to them, not me! Actually in one sense at least the situation may have become less dangerous because they are now able to tell you how to keep safe or at least how not to make it less safe.

Naturally, there is no guarantee that even at this early stage in the interactions Paul will respond as you would hope. In that case it is probably best to disengage – 'Paul, you need to leave now' – again simply repeating the same statement until he decides to go, or agrees to cooperate. Should this not prove sufficient or appropriate, then dear readers, all I can suggest is that the chapters that follow might help! Often, however, we do achieve the behaviour change that we are seeking, but just expect too much. If we ask Paul, for example, to step back and he steps back – even if it is only one step – it is enough. We shouldn't expect such a huge behavioural shift that he feels exposed, embarrassed or humiliated – it is enough that his behaviour has shifted in the desired direction. Indeed if we push for more right now, we might lose everything. At one level he will be aware that he is responding to our request, he just doesn't want his nose rubbed in it.

4 Manage Personal Boundaries

Now while I say that is enough, actually it isn't quite, because if we are to proceed with this interaction it has to continue in a respectful and appropriate manner. Although we will return to the management of personal boundaries in later chapters it is important to flag this up here. It seems to me that none of us are paid to be abused even though that quite clearly is a hazard that we may well encounter in the pursuit of our work. Professional boundaries, codes of ethics and practice, organizational policies and procedures, statutory requirements and so forth are not negotiable and in my view neither are personal boundaries. This is important, especially as we work in the 'people professions' and as such we have to use our own experience, resources, skills and personality in our work – these are our 'tools' so we should look after them. We all know when our personal boundaries have been violated, because we 'feel it'. Personally, I'm not a great fan of foul language, but I know many people who litter their language with obscenities and yet it doesn't bother me in the least – and this is because it is just idiomatic; it helps them express themselves and it is not used as a weapon to upset me or anyone else. However, I would find it difficult if they swore at me, or at anyone else – that would be upsetting and it may also have some implications for any further contact I have with the person who is now being abusive. Consequently, in this example, if Paul starts calling me names, for my own sake and for our future dealings, I will have to actively manage this. The tendency is, however, to confuse what we do in the main part of our work with that which is required during the crisis. If I had a client who went around calling me and my colleagues offensive names, I would want to sit down with them, confront them with their behaviour, help them to see the effect of their behaviour on others, show them how it isn't in their own best interests, discover what it is that makes them feel that they can be abusive to others and help them develop better, more effective and less abusive strategies in future. That, however, is after the crisis; during the crisis, when they may be pumped up, this is not appropriate and yet many professional will attempt this. Instead, once again, the rule is 'you don't do more, you do less, but you do something'. So if Paul turns on you and starts calling you names, you need to keep it really simple. The following would be ineffective and potentially escalating strategies: 'Please don't call me names, because I don't call you names'; 'Please don't call me names, because that will get you nowhere'; 'Please don't call me names, because it's not clever'. In each case we will have immediately given Paul a reflexive come back: 'I'm not like you!', 'I'm not going anywhere!', 'Are you calling me stupid?' It would be much better to stick simply with 'Please don't call me names' and no more. He may well carry on being abusive, we are not magicians, but at least in the process we can remain dignified and respectful and possibly he may get a sense that we feel secure enough in ourselves to hold our position without having to threaten him or put him down.

If Paul accepts our minimal demands – that is, he has raised his fist and we say 'Paul, put your hand down' and he puts it down just a bit – that's enough, we have his behaviour on track. Don't push for too much. Now we move into the final step of the de-escalation.

5 Defusing

The skills here are essentially those outlined in the section on defusing skills. Why does Paul, or anyone else get so angry? Because they feel at least at one level that they have been wronged. And what causes the behaviour to escalate? Usually the feeling that they are unable to communicate this effectively. In my cheese story, I felt wronged by my housemate, but it was his wilful refusal of my communication that led to the rapid escalation. Similarly, no doubt Paul wanted to express his dissatisfaction but it came out wrong. Whatever, with reactive aggression a breakdown of communication is almost always implicated at some level. The previous steps have been designed to return the situation to a point where effective communication can once again take place. So this is the next step. Once we have been able to get Paul's attention and slowed him down, set the conditions for safe engagement, assertively offered assistance, managed our personal boundaries and effected some positive, if minimal change in his behaviour – now we are ready to attend. This is where we begin to return to some of the core skills that most of us will feel we have a greater familiarity with. These are in turn, listening, summarizing, problem-solving and referral skills.

Now throughout this section I have been using Paul's behaviour in the group as our example – and up to this point a similar approach for these front-end skills would be appropriate almost regardless of the person we are dealing with because we are neither trying to 'solve the problem' nor 'trying to reason'. However, at this point although I will continue to use Paul's behaviour as our example, how you might apply these attending skills will vary from client to client. Obviously the way in which you may communicate with a pre-school child, a young person with learning disabilities, an adult with mental health issues and an older person with dementia will differ. The principles, however, remain the same. If Paul is standing, the first thing is to tell him to take a seat in a way that conveys that he will have your undivided attention: 'Paul, please sit down. Talk to me.' From here on in the important thing is to demonstrate good listening skills and make sure that we bite our tongue every time we wish to correct, challenge or put across our own view. It is not the task of this book to teach good communication skills, which should be the core of any helping professional's repertoire, but a few points are worth highlighting. Open-ended questions involving interrogative words such as who, where, when, what and how are fine, but it is better to avoid questions involving the word 'why'. The reason for this is that it is relatively easy for the person you are dealing with to answer the who-where-when-what-how questions by simply reporting on what they can recall. The 'why' question, however, requires a higher level of analysis and that may prove taxing and embarrassing if they are still in a state of agitation or if they have impaired problem-solving skills. Our task here is to allow them to express safely whatever it is they have to express while at the same time reducing the tension. It is not necessary for us to agree with what they have to communicate, only that we clearly convey a willingness to receive that communication. So if Paul says, 'The reason I am so angry is that I was told that if I attended these groups sessions for a month, I would have my tag removed and I would be moved to the top of the housing list – and it hasn't happened so I've had a guts full of all this!', we don't respond with 'I think you have got the wrong end of the stick here, Paul' or 'Have you any idea how long the housing list is?' or 'Don't you think everyone would be signing up for anger management groups if it got them to the top of the housing list?' – all of which are a step too far. A less inflammatory response would be to accept the emotional message without necessarily agreeing or disagreeing with the factual one –

'Well Paul, I have to say that if someone made a promise to me and then didn't follow through, I might feel angry also.'

This can then be followed by further enquiries – who, when, what and so on. By now Paul should be considerably less agitated and it is advisable to give him as much time as possible to explain his situation. Once he has done that we can demonstrate that his message has been heard by summarizing:

'OK, I just want to check that I have understood this correctly. You say that you were led to believe that if you attended these sessions for a month you would be de-tagged and your name accelerated to the top of the housing list. Although you have found these sessions difficult you have stuck with them, only to discover that there are no changes to the conditions of your court order and that no one here has any control over the housing department. As a result you feel that you have been deceived and that is why you became so angry. Have I got that right, Paul?'

Assuming Paul accepts our summary there are just a couple more small steps before the de-escalation is complete. The first is to demonstrate that there will be a response to his issue. If it is something within our role and skills set we might handle it ourselves:

'OK Paul, if you can let me see that letter, I'll see if I can get to the bottom of this.'

Or if it is not within our role, we should take some responsibility for referring it on to the appropriate professionals:

'OK Paul, would you like me to call your probation officer now to find out what has happened?'

The second and final step is to thank Paul for explaining the situation and if it feels appropriate to explore alternative strategies for dealing with similar situations that might arise in the future: 'I appreciate the fact that you have been able to explain this to me. I'm sure, however, that you are aware that this has affected other group members too. Have you any thoughts about how . . .?'

So there it is. Very simple as long as we keep it simple. There is no magic and there are no guarantees that if you follow a 'script' like that above it will always lead to a de-escalation, but even if it doesn't, it provides us with some direction and an alternative to chaos and panic. Indeed if we can practise keeping things simple in these 'lower level' or escalating crises, we may well be doing the groundwork for the rapid reaction skills required for managing ourselves and the behaviour of the aggressor when they reach the pivotal point.

Summary

We have looked at some of the key themes and principles in dealing with difficult reactive aggression and then highlighted two sets of skills – defusing skills and de-escalating skills. Defusing skills are essentially an extension of the good customer care skills which hopefully most readers will be very familiar with are appropriate for responding to service users who may be upset, angry or in some other way emotionally charged but are still some way off becoming violent. De-escalating skills are on the same behavioural trajectory as defusing skills but are used when the service user is at risk of arriving at the pivotal point and potentially losing control. These are front-end skills which aim to return the service user to the point where defusing skills can be used. In the next two chapters we will explore what happens when the pivotal point for reactive aggression is reached.

Top Tips
- When dealing with escalating behaviour the rule is always the same – 'you don't do more, you do less, but you always must do something'. The more dangerous the behaviour, the more important this will be – make this your mantra.
- At this pre-pivotal point level, as long as your attitude is right and you are doing something, your non-verbal behaviour will manage itself – you do not have to micro-manage non-verbal behaviours such as eye contact, body posture, hand movements, etc.

- The important point is to convey rather than say, and for the aggressor to sense rather than think. This provides 'under-the-radar' communications that involve little loss of face and that are also difficult to resist or reject.
- You should become familiar with both the defusing and de-escalation process. As front-end skills they are appropriate in many situations and can therefore be practised and refined.
- These de-escalation skills are on the same behavioural trajectory as the rapid reaction skills that will be introduced in the following chapters. Consequently the greater your competence at this level, the better prepared you will be for the more serious crises that we will be exploring next.

Chapter Four
Dangerous Reactive Aggression
A Case Study

In this chapter you will:
- work through a detailed case study of a real incident as if you are the professional involved
- reflect on how you might think, feel and respond to the events as they evolve
- clarify the issues and concerns that the case study raises for you in your practice
- compare your experience with that of the actual professional involved
- consider the story from the service user's perspective

This will help you assess the rapid reaction skills identified in Chapter 5.

The 'Walk-Through' Case Studies

This chapter begins with the first of our 'walk-through' case studies in which we will be working through real incidents in the way they would be experienced in real time, without the benefit of hindsight but with all the complex interweaving layers of information that in professional practice can both illuminate and distract. I suggest that you read through the case study imagining that you are the worker involved – reflecting, as you go along, on your thoughts, feelings and actions. Questions are asked along the way to assist with this. Try not to skip ahead – there have been a lot of advances in professional practice over the past few decades but time travel is not one of them!

Note
Some professional groups do not have as much background information as presented here, especially if their role is investigative or enforcing. In such cases, you can start the story at the section 'At the scene'. (p. 83)

After you have worked through the incident you will be told the rest of the story, first from the professional's viewpoint and then from that of the service user. This will be followed by a commentary which will highlight some of the key practice issues. Finally in the following chapter this example will be used to introduce the rapid reaction skills necessary to influence reactive aggression when it arrives at the dysphoric crisis.

The Barclay Family

It's 9.30 on a cold winter morning and you are approaching the Barclay household, a well-kept terraced house on a large housing estate. Mrs Barclay, 42, and her daughter Donna, 19, should be expecting you. There hadn't been any particular cause for concern on your three previous visits and on each occasion you got the impression that Mrs Barclay, a rather anxious and agitated woman, would give up her whole day in anticipation of your visit. Donna, on the other hand was forthright, outspoken, even confrontational. On your first visit, when you were accompanied by a colleague, this had been a little unsettling but Donna mellowed considerably once she realized that you were there to help them.

Although this will only be your fourth visit, in that short time you've got to know the Barclays quite well. They are a white, British single-parent family who moved into the area four years ago. They had to leave their home town quickly and this had been facilitated by Social Services, the Police and the Housing Department. For years little had been known about them. The father was a long distance lorry driver and often away on long-haul trips. The mother, Mrs Barclay, was seldom seen in public, and the daughter, Donna, had been doing well at school. It was around the age of 13 that things began to change. Teachers noticed that Donna's school work was falling off and she seemed to lose interest in her studies. Often she was distant and inattentive in class, and when challenged could become abusive. She was also getting into fights with other pupils and would often be absent from school without explanation. The Educational Welfare Service found it extremely hard to engage with her at any level and her mother appeared to deny that there was a problem.

Shortly after her 15th birthday, late at night, Donna was found crouched over and badly injured in a local park. She was taken to A&E by ambulance and treated there. She had sustained cuts to the face and body, severe bruising, fractured and broken bones and some damage to her internal organs. She claimed that she had been sniffing glue and got on the wrong end of a fight with a gang from the local estate. The staff at the hospital, however, identified many other earlier, untreated and unexplained injuries indicating that this was far from the first time that she had been assaulted. There were no signs of sexual assault but there were what appeared to be self-inflicted cuts to both arms. At this point social services and the police were alerted.

Investigations started, but Mrs Barclay would say nothing, Mr Barclay's whereabouts were unknown and Donna was sticking to her story. It was only when the social workers said that they were worried for her safety and couldn't allow her to return home that Donna told the full story – but only on condition that they promised to protect her mother.

Donna's father would be away, sometimes for a few days, sometimes for weeks or months, but Donna said she could always sense when he was about to return. There would be an 'atmosphere' about the house. Her mother would be in a state of panic, flying off the hook at the smallest thing. Everything about the house had to be cleaned, checked and re-checked. Meanwhile Donna would look on helplessly. When her father's truck pulled up outside, her mother would send Donna to her room and tell her to shut the door, or she would be given some money and told to go to the cinema with a friend. Her father would start drinking, criticizing his wife and blaming her for everything that was wrong in his life. Mrs Barclay's attempts to appease her husband only infuriated him and violence was almost always the end result. By the age of 13 Donna could no longer hold back and in spite of her mother's pleas would challenge her father – resulting in the violence being turned on her. After the assaults Donna would run from the house and hang out with the gangs on the estate, in the squats or sleep rough. When her father's truck left, she would return home. Donna and her mother never talked about it, but the pattern continued until the day Donna was admitted to hospital.

Both Donna and her mother feared for their lives. Donna went to stay briefly with a foster carer while her mother went to a women's refuge. The police were unable to apprehend the father and so it was eventually decided to relocate Donna and her mother for their own safety. They moved into the council house which you are now visiting, some 120 miles from their home town. Donna left school at 16 refusing all help offered by the school and social services, but demanding help for her mother. She eventually got a job at a local supermarket. Her mother who is largely house-bound has been supported by the local Community Mental Health Team through a community psychiatric nurse who visits weekly. The only other agency involved until recently has been the Housing Association managing the property in which they now live. For the past couple of years they have been good tenants, paying their rent on time and keeping themselves to themselves.

Seven months ago, however, the Housing Association noticed that they were falling behind with the rent and substantial arrears were building up. Letters went unanswered and phone calls were promptly put down. Eventually a housing officer went to visit the property to see if they could help but no one was in. Further enquiries were made and it was discovered that Mrs Barclay had been admitted to an acute psychiatric ward and Donna had been arrested, charged and placed on remand.

It appears that Mrs Barclay was pregnant and when Donna discovered this she started spending the rent money on expensive items for the baby. She told her mother that she could afford it because she had been awarded a pay rise. The spending spun out of control and Donna realized that soon her mother would find out. In desperation and heavily under the influence of alcohol she broke into the supermarket where she worked. She was caught in the act on CCTV and within an hour the police went to the house to arrest her. Still heavily intoxicated, however, she resisted arrest and assaulted one of the police officers. Her mother meanwhile became increasingly distraught and had to be detained under the Mental Health Act for her own safety and that of the unborn child.

Three months ago Mrs Barclay was assessed to be well enough to return home. She now has the support of a social worker, housing officer, support worker, CPN, midwife and a home carer and appears to be coping. A month later Donna was allowed to return home on probation and also had a number of helping professionals involved – a probation officer, a youth offending team worker and a support worker from a local drugs and alcohol service.

For the purposes of this case study, you are one of these professionals. This is your fourth visit. The first visit you made jointly with a colleague to assess any risks. Since then you have been visiting alone and at the end of each visit you make an appointment for your return. Mrs Barclay is always ready for you and indeed it appears that she will have spent hours prior to your arrival spring cleaning the property. Sometimes she opens the door and sometimes it is Donna, but even then Mrs Barclay will be looking out of the window in anxious anticipation. Mrs Barclay feels responsible for not protecting Donna when she was younger and constantly worries about not being a fit mother. This annoys Donna who repeatedly tells her 'not to talk like that or they won't let you keep the baby'. Although angry and frustrated she quickly calms down and apologizes by saying, 'I'm sorry, I know I'm a bit mouthy, I don't mean nothing by it'. You've noticed that Donna finds it hard to talk about herself and when pushed responds by saying, 'You ain't my effing shrink, so back off'. Again, she will quickly calm down and apologize. She feels embarrassed that she has let her mother and herself down and is determined to put things right. She also tells you she has stopped drinking.

After the second visit you got the sense that Donna wanted to say something to you, but might be holding back because she was embarrassed to do so in front of her mother. Consequently, at the end of your last visit you asked if Donna would show you to the door and took this opportunity to ask if there was anything else bothering her. She says she wants to pay back the rent and has worked out that by saving the money she would have spent on drink she can afford to pay £10.00 maybe £15.00 per week extra – but is worried that if the Housing Association get difficult she might 'blow her top'. You said that it sounds like a reasonable offer and would be happy to make some informal enquiries for her. She goes on to say that she is also frightened that social services might be planning to take the baby away. You did your best to explain that every effort would be made to support her mother to keep the baby and that care proceedings would be the absolute last option. She responded with, 'It's just doing my head in – I've had social workers lie to me all my effing life, but you're a professional – they'd be straight with you'. You agreed to talk to the child and family team but explained that they may not be able to talk to you. With that you agreed to return the following Friday at 9.30. She thanked you and seemed greatly relieved.

You made a couple of calls and it was clear that her proposal to restructure the rent payments was acceptable and that the child and family team had no intention of removing the baby. You tried ringing the Barclays on a couple of occasions to pass this on, but there was no answer. You are aware that Mrs Barclay must be coming very close to full term. In addition you will be going on holiday straight after your visit on Friday and so need to tell the Barclays that your colleague Zowie will fill in while you are away.

With everything in place you head off to visit the Barclay family on Friday morning as agreed. You have a clear agenda: to reassure Donna regarding the rent repayments and her concerns about social services and the baby; to let Donna and her mother know that you will be going on holiday; to wish them well; to make sure that they have the support they need should Mrs Barclay go into hospital over the weekend; to let them know about Zowie and assess their reactions.

On the surface, it's just another visit. Mrs Barclay and Donna should be expecting you. You know them and have good news. You did a full risk assessment following your first visit and this had raised no serious concerns. You just need to wrap this up before going on holiday.

At the Scene

You approach the property, a well-kept terraced house on a large housing estate. As you approach you notice that the curtains upstairs and down haven't been opened, but it is still only 9.30 a.m. There is loud music emanating from the upstairs – nothing to make you think that there is a wild party in progress but loud enough to bother neighbours.

> What are your thoughts at this stage? How do you think you would be feeling? What would you do next?

You approach the front door and are about to knock when a neighbour from the adjacent property appears in his dressing gown. He starts remonstrating, 'Are you going there? Are you going to have words with them? That racket's been going on since midnight!' You say that you are sorry that they have been inconvenienced and will see if you can have a word. 'A word!! You sort them out or I will!' comes the reply. You say that there is no need for that, you appreciate how annoying this must be but it is better not to get involved. You say that if you get no joy you will inform the neighbourhood warden. The neighbour, muttering under his breath, grudgingly returns to his house. As he does, you call back and ask if this happens a lot. The answer is, no, he is aware that there was some sort of trouble with the police a few months back but other than that you would hardly know that anyone lived there. He goes on to mention that the noise started about midnight and he couldn't believe the names he'd been called. You can see that the neighbour is getting over-wrought so thank him and suggest he returns to his house while you investigate.

> What are your options at this point?

You press the bell and then knock on the door. You are aware of some movement inside and so move closer to the door to assess what is going on inside. The volume of the music drops and you can hear someone coming to the door. The door is unlatched and slowly opened. There is a young woman, maybe late teens or early 20s. You have never seen her before. She looks a bit glazed and keeps wiping her nose. She is white, with wild black and purple hair, black lipstick, black fingernails and black clothing. She has a welcoming smile and asks, 'What do you want?' You explain who you are and that you should be expected. She replies 'You'd better come in then.' She invites you into the front room. She tells you to make yourself at home while she lets them know that you are here.

> Would you enter the property? If not, why and what would you do instead?

You are scanning the area for any clues, but the place is remarkably clean, tidy and devoid of any sign of disorder – there are no needles, cans, or any indication that there are any other unexpected people in the property. You take a seat in the voluminous sofa and have to re-adjust yourself on the frame to avoid being swallowed up. The young woman leaves the room. You rapidly scan the room – there are some empty cans of strong lager in the bin but the surfaces are clean.

As you collect your thoughts you hear some movement outside. You are aware that the only exit is the door by which you entered. The sound of activity outside in the hall is increasing but indistinct. You could walk out but you don't know what is awaiting you on the other side of the door.

> How would you be feeling now? What do you think is going on? What are your options?

The Incident

Bear in mind that what follows all takes place within about two minutes from beginning to end and is rapidly changing by the second.

There's a click, then the door bursts open, and suddenly there's a bloodied figure standing over you. It's Donna. She's staring right at you with wild, dilated red eyes. She has a blood soaked tea towel wrapped around one arm, and is sweating profusely. She's not saying anything but her breathing is fast and heavy and the muscles around her face are twitching. It feels like anything – the wrong look, wrong words, wrong move – could set her off.

> How do you imagine you would be reacting physically and emotionally at this point? Have you any ideas about how you might respond?

She continues staring right at you, although there's little recognition in her eyes and her breathing is getting faster. Suddenly she picks up a dining chair and throws it across the room. She is screaming now, no words, just noise. She kicks over a glass coffee table which smashes leaving sharp shards of glass everywhere. She is standing right over you now – within arm's length. You are aware of the smell of stale alcohol on her breath and the hot sweat from her body. She's shaking with rage, but still hasn't said anything.

The situation is changing faster than you can think. What can you do? Should you return her gaze or look away? Should you say anything or try to ride the storm?

She starts shouting at you. 'You effing whore', 'You care for cash!', 'You've effed up!', 'I hate you!', 'It's all effed up!', 'You're nothing!' As the torrent of abuse continues she is rapidly getting more and more wound up and out of control. Suddenly a large knife appears from under the tea towel and she's holding it to your throat: 'You're going to pay!' Her hand is shaking and there's blood on the knife.

What are you thinking? Do you think this is about you or do you think this would be happening to anyone who crossed Donna's path at this moment?

Still looking straight at you she picks up the overturned dining chair and sits on it. Suddenly she turns the knife on herself cutting deeply into her arm. At the same time she is screaming, 'What are you gonna do?' She's looking wild and pumped up. 'Do something then!' 'You're effing useless!' 'You ain't got an effing clue!' The cuts are deep and blood is everywhere.

Do you think that the fact that she has turned the knife on herself makes you any less in danger? Would you try to stop her harming herself further? How? What are the risks?

Suddenly she's standing over you again pointing the knife at you. The screaming continues, and then everything goes quiet. Still staring at you she moves the knife towards her own face and draws the knife across it. Blood comes rushing out. There's blood all over you by now. Then she starts laughing at you – manic, delirious, maybe psychotic – but before you know it the knife is pointing at you again.

Do you think she is running out of steam or building up to something worse?

She's screaming at you to get up. She's still standing over you holding the knife and she still seems out of control. She screams, 'Get up!' repeatedly, each time getting louder and moving closer to you. There's no room to get up and even if you could you would move even closer to the knife.

> What do you think she means by 'Get up!' – an invitation to leave, a taunt or provocation, an invitation to a fight, or maybe Donna doesn't know herself? How might you respond?

Suddenly she lunges at you, pulling you roughly out of the sofa by your clothes which are ripped. You feel something sharp and she bundles you out of the room into the hall and then out onto the street. You are aware that you have been cut.

> What do you do next?
>
> Now that you are away from it, what do think had happened before your arrival and why had Donna suddenly become so dangerous?
>
> On reflection, given the speed and violence of the incident, do you think there is anything you could have done differently?

The Professional's Story

The above story is closely based on a real incident, obviously adapted to protect the identities of those involved. Having reflected on your own experience, I will now tell the story from the perspective of the professional, who I shall call Pat, that visited the Barclay family on that day. Because this book is really about you, assume that Pat is the same age, gender and culture as you, and does the same job (although this section is written as if Pat is female). Obviously with hindsight Pat might have handled things differently but hindsight is a luxury we don't have. We operate in real time with all the complexities and differing pressures that brings.

For Pat this visit was expected to be quite routine. There had already been a risk assessment, Pat knew the Barclays, and the visit should not only be expected but welcomed. If a child was going to be removed, someone was to be detained under the Mental Health Act, a court order served, or if Pat was bringing bad news, then there would be good reason to be concerned. This, however, was a largely goodwill visit and Pat genuinely wished the Barclays well.

Pat did, however, say that she felt something was wrong on arrival outside the house but then rationalized the feeling. There was the loud music, the closed curtains, the angry neighbour and at the door an unexpected guest – but some people always play their music loud, don't get up until two o'clock in the afternoon, are always rowing with their neighbours and constantly have friends around. For Pat, if those were reasons not to visit then she wouldn't be visiting half her caseload. Anyhow, it would feel difficult to hand the case over to Zowie without even having mentioned to the Barclays that this was to happen.

The neighbour appeared as an unnecessary and unwelcome hindrance and so was dispatched as quickly as possible. Clearly, however, something was up and Pat was curious and wanted to investigate. Pat didn't want to go on holiday worrying about what had been left behind, and also felt a responsibility to hand the case over to Zowie. Although feeling some anxiety in approaching the property, the young woman at the door was welcoming and gave little clue as to what was to follow. Furthermore, as Pat scanned the property there was nothing to raise concern – there wasn't a party going on and if there had been it was over by now. The property was clean and tidy and there didn't appear to be anyone about that would raise concerns.

Nonetheless, Pat felt uncomfortable. In the front room there appeared be nothing of concern. Feeling confused Pat agreed to take a seat while trying to figure out what was going on. Her anxiety grew as she started to wonder where Mrs Barclay was, and why Donna, normally so protective of her mother, would play her music so loud. The empty cans and the sounds from outside increased the tension, but the more Pat thought about it, the available options rapidly diminished. Running now might just mean running straight into trouble. Maybe it was a lot of fuss over nothing? Things are rarely as bad as you fear, surely? It's too late now anyway.

Suddenly as the door burst open, Pat jolted back into the sofa, muscles tensing, desperately holding breath for fear of letting out a scream. At first it was hard to realize that this was Donna. Desperately Pat tried to control her facial muscles, not wishing to show how alarmed she was. Where to look? Returning Donna's gaze might show that she was paying attention and taking Donna seriously. Equally the 'look' in Donna's eyes might help 'read' the situation. On the other hand, it might also make her the focus of Donna's rage, draw Donna on or be misinterpreted as a challenge. Looking away might convey a non-confrontational, submissive stance, but what if Donna saw it as ignorant, dismissive or incompetent? Pat felt like saying something, but couldn't think what.

The screaming and furniture being flung around the room pushed Pat further back into the devouring sofa. The words were indistinct, but the actions were rapidly escalating. There was no time to think, the fear and panic taking over everything. When the knife came out, Pat felt everything go still inside. All Pat could do was to hold on tight and hope. When Donna turned the knife on herself, Pat was horrified and wanted to stop her and call out, 'Please don't!' but the words wouldn't come out. When she cut her face and laughed Pat felt terrified and helpless. Maybe up to this point Pat felt that if there was any hope, it was that they had a relationship – but this wasn't the Donna that Pat knew. When she screamed 'Get up!' Pat didn't see this as an invitation to leave but a challenge. The more Donna screamed the more rigid and frightened Pat became. Fearing that inactivity was being read as resistance and enraging Donna further, Pat tried getting up only for her whole body to start convulsing. Suddenly Donna attacked.

Once outside the property Pat called for an ambulance and the police, and then their manager. Pat wasn't aware of the cut until the ambulance arrived – thinking that the blood on her clothes belonged to Donna not herself.

Donna's Story

This visit took place on the Friday. On the Monday, Donna's mother had gone into hospital giving birth to a baby boy late on Tuesday night. The baby's arrival raised her level of anxiety enormously – would she be able to cope, would she be a good enough mother? For Donna, however, it was a moment of great hope. Maybe a lot of things had gone wrong in her life, but at least she could make sure her baby brother would get a better deal. She could imagine telling her brother to work hard at school, to stay out of trouble, to help those who are less fortunate. She could imagine taking him out to the local park and the bond that would develop between them. The arrival of the baby provided Donna with a feeling of hope for the future.

At the hospital there was a concern about Mrs Barclay's level of anxiety and she was given medication to help her cope. On the Thursday she was discharged home with the baby. Donna wanted to show her mother that she could be relied on to help and so spent much of the day caring and bonding with her baby brother. Late that night she could hear the baby crying in her mother's bedroom and went up to see if she could help. When she got there she discovered that her mother was unconscious and there were empty packets of pills on the floor. Despite her frantic attempts she was unable to rouse her. Donna had sold her mobile phone to help pay back the rent money and so she had to leave the house in search of a pay phone, knowing that as each second passed her mother could already have died and her baby brother was alone. She made the emergency call, but was panicking because it seemed to take so long. She ran back to the house but as she re-entered the street where she lived she saw an ambulance already parked outside. She had left the front door open and now the ambulance driver and paramedic were taking her mother out of the house on a stretcher and into the ambulance. She watched in disbelief hoping she would wake up soon and realize it was just a bad dream. Then to her horror she saw the paramedic covering her mother's face with a sheet. The other paramedic returned to the house and collected the baby. Donna was too stunned and frightened to go up to them, and watched as the ambulance left.

She returned to the house raging at herself – why didn't she spot anything? Why didn't she go to the ambulance? – and the world – why do bad things always happen to me? Why don't I ever get a break? Why did mum have to take that overdose? Up until now Donna never played her music loud as she knew it would upset her mother – but now she was dead and the baby was gone. She put her music on loud and started drinking, but she couldn't blot it out. She started cutting herself to avoid being overwhelmed by the emotional pain. The next door neighbour called round to ask her to turn the music down but withdrew very quickly when he saw the state Donna was in. The young woman called round in search of drugs and was apparently completely stoned. It's not clear what happened between her and Donna, but what is clear is that Donna didn't want to see Pat or any other professional – she didn't want them to tell her that her mother was dead, or ask her why she didn't spot anything, or why she wasn't there when the ambulance called. Nor did she want anyone to see her in the state she was in. So when the young woman let Pat in and told Donna that there was someone to see her in the front room, not realizing how out of control she was, she stormed into the front room with the knife she had been using to cut herself hidden in the tea towel. She thought she would just tell Pat to go, but when she burst in no words came out. Because Pat was saying nothing, it was if a huge empty chasm existed between them, with each passing second increasing the pressure to do something. Suddenly the pressure was too much and she lashed out, going increasingly out of control and dangerous. Each act was a desperate attempt to buy time or an attempt to provoke Pat into action and so take the pressure off Donna. She had little idea of how frightened Pat was, assuming that Pat was used to being in situations like this and maybe that helping professionals are given an inoculation against fear. Her focus was on her own world as it was falling apart, not Pat's. So when she said 'Get up!' she actually meant get up and get out before something really bad happens. Pat was an unwanted audience that simply wouldn't go away. Not understanding Pat's inactivity, she attacked.

Commentary

Here we will critically dissect the incident. The purpose is not to confer blame on Pat, who was one of the two victims in this incident, but to see what can be learned for future good practice.

Risk Assessment and Lone-working

Pat didn't see this as a difficult, and certainly not a dangerous visit. Indeed on the balance of probabilities it is far more likely that Donna would have been delighted with the news about the rent and social services – and perhaps because of this there were many missed opportunities. Appropriately a thorough risk assessment had been undertaken when Pat first started to work with the Barclay family. That assessment, however, was undertaken with the facts as they were known at the time and could not take into account the changing circumstances. I never saw the risk assessment and so I can't comment on how rigorous it was and whether there were any specific concerns raised, but it was interpreted as 'it is safe for Pat to visit on their own'. Most of us want to see the best in the people we work with – and here, understandably Pat was encouraged by the positive developments in her relationship with Donna and was keen to provide her with good news. Nonetheless, looked at more dispassionately there clearly were risks.

First, the best predictor of future violence is past violence. Donna had both been on the receiving end of a great deal of violence and had assaulted a police officer – importantly, in her own home. Furthermore, Pat had first hand experience that not only could Donna react aggressively, but that her moods could fluctuate rapidly. Add to this that Donna had told Pat that she could easily lose it if confronted with a situation that she didn't know how to handle, and we have a highly inflammable concoction. Finally, whatever we know about Donna generally this is a critical period in her life – she is trying hard to prove herself to her mother, to stay off the drink and drugs, to cope with the involvement of all the helping services, and her mother is soon to give birth. This should be a time of great caution.

On arriving at the property Pat sensed that something was wrong. This is the first kind of warning coming from the body referred to in Chapter 2: the thalamus picking up the danger and activating the body via the limbic system before the frontal cortex has caught up with the developing situation. This should have alerted Pat to the need to re-evaluate the situation. First off, if visiting clients in their home, it is advisable to have their phone or mobile number. Then Pat could have stepped back and given the Barclays a courtesy call and checked that it was still convenient to call around. On the phone Pat could have clarified the purpose of the call, assessed whether Donna sounded coherent and amenable and even checked her compliance by politely asking if she could turn the music down. In fact, it is good practice to give a courtesy call in advance of all home visits – it confers respect and also avoids embarrassing situations at the door when the client may have forgotten about the visit and may have something in the property they would rather we don't see.

In this case, because Donna had sold her phone, this wasn't an option. It might, however, be advisable to call any other professionals involved with the Barclay family – they may have been able to alert Pat to the more recent developments. Alternatively, Pat could have called her manager or a colleague to talk through their rising concerns. When the neighbour came out, it is understandable that Pat didn't want them to interfere, but they could have been a valuable source of information.

The loud music, the unopened curtains and the angry neighbour don't in themselves indicate danger – indeed in some households this can be the norm. The salient point, however, was that everything was different and so Pat should have proceeded as if this was a 'cold call' without a previous assessment. Pat should, therefore, have approached this visit as if it were for the first time – or withdrawn, may be putting a note through the letterbox indicating that she had called and how to get in touch. Understandably, however, Pat was concerned for the Barclays and didn't feel she could hand the case over to Zowie without seeing them first.

Pat knocked on the door, and then moved closer to see if she could hear what was going on inside. Good practice, however, would be to move away from the door after knocking on it. This avoids giving the impression that we are trying to push our way in, and also provides more space for an exit, should the service user be agitated or if they have a dog. When the young woman arrived at the door there was an opportunity to ask her whether both Mrs Barclay and Donna were in and to ascertain whether there was anyone else in the house. When invited in, Pat could have politely declined and asked for Mrs Barclay to come to the door.

Entering the property, Pat was looking out for indications of danger, perhaps to confirm what she was feeling in her body. Unfortunately violence doesn't follow the stereotypes and happens in country mansions as well as dingy squats. If Pat felt that something was wrong she would have been better advised to withdraw rather than investigate. On entering the front room, Pat sat down to steady herself, which is understandable, but being seated restricts options and it would be better to wait until invited by the householder. In fact at this point Pat hadn't even established who it was that the young woman was going to get – Mrs Barclay or Donna. Enquiring about this may give further clues and even an opportunity to leave: 'You know what, it's not that important, here's my card. Just let them know they can call me before 5.30 if they want.'

The Incident

Tragic though Donna's story is, Pat would only know this after the event. All Pat could know was what she experienced. The pivotal point, the dysphoric crisis occurred at the point that Donna burst into the room. The intense and immediate reaction within Pat's body left no doubt about that. At that point Pat suddenly was aware that she was in great danger. This was not a moment for defusing or de-escalating but for rapid reaction. Up to the point of bursting into the room Donna may well have believed that she might handle the situation – 'Get out, sling your hook!' – but the moment she burst into the room, high on alcohol and drugs, emotions pumping, suddenly there were no words. Moments might seem like an eternity and Donna was left in a psychological vacuum. Pat wanted to react or respond but could find nothing that might not provoke an even more violent response. In the absence of any response from Pat, the onus fell on Donna to do something. The throwing of the furniture was just a desperate attempt to do something, to buy some time maybe in hope of finding a way through what would seem like an impossible situation. The problem was, once started it was difficult to see how to stop. Some might feel that the expression of her rage through smashing the furniture might be cathartic, but as we saw earlier the evidence goes the other way – that the expression of violence generates further violence.

Perhaps even before Donna had started throwing the furniture, Pat was experiencing the full effects of the acute stress response and had entered into a state on tonic immobility – she was frozen. From this point on there was little that Pat could do other than hold tight and ride the storm. It is, however, instructive to examine how the crisis developed. Immediately after the furniture was thrown, Donna started calling Pat names. I remember a common saying 'Sticks and stones may break my bones, but names will never hurt me' from my childhood. This is, however, not the whole story. Not only is the psychological pain often much worse than the physical pain in the long term but the act of name-calling depersonalizes the victim and makes them easier to attack. The consequence of not intervening was to leave Donna to fill each passing moment, and it doesn't take a great deal of insight to observe that the worst of all worlds is to be controlled by someone who is completely out of control. Each ensuing act probably had little individual significance – they just bought fragments of time. If Donna was out of control, by definition she could not put herself back in control. When the knife appeared the risk escalated exponentially. Donna probably had no idea what she would do with the knife, but the longer it was there, the more likely it was that something would go wrong. No one would be able to predict that she would suddenly turn the knife on herself, probably not even Donna. This could very easily be mistaken for the deliberate self-harm that she engaged in the night before and was noticed when she attended A&E all those years ago. Actually it was a desperate taunt, an act designed to get Pat to do something to take the pressure off Donna. When she turned the knife on her face and then laughed it was the point of no return and this was no longer the Donna that Pat had any knowledge of.

When Donna screamed 'Get up!', any hope of holding tight and riding the storm disappeared. This perhaps is a very clear demonstration of how ineffective the frontal cortex is in these situations. One would think that there can't be much confusion between two words, but when your life depends on it, 'Get up!' can mean 'get up and leave', 'get up and let's finish this', or 'get up and I don't know what I'm saying'. By default or commission, Pat will now have to take the consequences – and that is what happened.

This incident could have occurred without the warnings and opportunities available to her. Everything could have been as normal with Mrs Barclay inviting Pat in, offering a seat and then going to put the kettle on – only for Donna to arrive through the back entrance and burst in on Pat. Of course we should do all we can to minimize the risk, but what happens when that is not possible? Now we are in the domain of rapid reaction skills, which will be the focus of the next chapter.

> ### Exercise
> This story is told with Donna as a young white woman, but take a moment to reconsider what would be different if Donna was male, older or of a different ethnic background.

The issues around race and ethnicity are reviewed briefly in Chapter 6, while below some of the issues around gender are raised.

Gender Issues and Violence

It is undeniable that gender plays a huge role in relation to violence. In some psychiatric wards there is a tacit agreement to send in female staff when trouble breaks out because it is believed that they have a more calming influence and better interpersonal skills. Conversely in other settings it is always the men that go rushing in. Either way it is an ethically dubious practice but one that stems from a realization that gender differences are highly significant. It is undoubtedly true that men would feel very differently to women visiting a female prison, and the converse would also be true of women visiting a male prison. Some of this will be due to physical factors (including hormonal differences), child rearing differences, differential social role expectations, social skills and so forth. There is a huge amount of literature on men and violence and on the violence that men perpetrate on women, but relatively little on violence perpetrated by women. In fact Buss (1961) claimed that women are so rarely aggressive that there was little point in studying it! Later reviewers, e.g. Björkqvist and Niemelä (1992), are less convinced that gender plays a significant role in the incidence of aggression, but suggest that female aggression is often expressed differently and less directly. Meichembaum (2006) agrees that girls tend to use 'more indirect, social and verbal forms of aggression' such as social exclusion, rumour spreading, name calling and teasing. This is most likely to occur in same-sex peer groups. Conversely, boys are twice as likely to engage in direct physical aggression.

Of course one of the problems in extrapolating from these studies is that the service users encountered by helping professionals (e.g. survivors of domestic violence, offenders, young people in care, mental health service clients, etc.) may not mirror the general population. Clearly there needs to a lot more research into the nature of female violence.

Summary

Working through the case study outlined in this chapter will have raised many questions for you. Clearly the outcome of the incident involving Donna was catastrophic and in the next chapter we will be examining exactly what skills might be appropriate to deal with such fast-flowing and dangerous behaviour.

Chapter Five

Skills for Responding to
Dangerous Reactive Aggression
Rapid Reactions

In this chapter you will:
- explore the nature of reactive aggression as it escalates towards the perpetrating levels and the dysphoric crisis
- identify front-end rapid reaction skills at each of the three stages involved in responding to fast-flowing and highly reactive behaviour
- learn about how knowledge of concepts such as dissociation, implied suggestions, under-the-radar skills, line of least resistance, empathy and the Stockholm syndrome can be used to tilt the behaviour away from violence

Imagine . . .
Donna crashes through the door, covered in blood, sweating profusely, eyes raging, and a look of murder on her face. You jolt back, shocked and startled. There's a knife. The room suddenly feels much smaller, your muscles tighten, you go hot and sweaty. Desperately you try to control your body, the look on your face, your shaking hand. Your mind goes blank and your body rebels . . .

This is your crisis and Donna's crisis. The crisis is not between you and Donna, but within each of you. Within seconds, however, the crisis will engulf the two of you – and what happens in those seconds might radically change the course of events.

The chances of accurately working out what is going on with Donna and calibrating your own finely tuned response are minimal. It is doubtful that even Donna really knew what was happening or why – much less what it would take to return her to safety. Even if we could understand what was going on, it may not help – right now, this second. To make the point more strongly, let me give you the advantage of hindsight together with full knowledge of Donna's story and all the time that you need to consider how best to respond. How confident are you that your brain and body will combine effectively to produce your carefully thought-out plan as Donna bursts through the door and lunges at you?

The point at which Donna bursts into the lounge is the point where most texts leave off. This is for good reason. Common sense also suggests we foreclose on any advice at this point, because how can you, for example, even at the most basic level, stop yourself from freezing when you didn't realize you would freeze until you froze! And then it is clearly too late! This is the realm where you will be told 'there are no rules', 'every situation is different', 'you won't know how you will react until you are there', and so on. This is also the point that the previous four chapters have been preparing us for – the pivotal point for reactive aggression – the dysphoric crisis. We have to go back to our model of understanding how the brain and body combine when under threat to begin to see a way through this conundrum. The conundrum is 'how can you respond safely, taking control of your body, when you have to do so faster than you can think and where there is no margin for error?' It sounds like an impossible task but only if you approach the problem in the traditional way.

In order to make this more manageable, I am going to break down the response to immediate and overwhelming danger into three steps. In each we need to discover skills that will help us manage what is going on within us while simultaneously containing the danger coming from the aggressor. First we need to engage in a way that is safe and manageable and takes the pressure to act off the aggressor. This has to be done in a way that will not cause our body to rebel. Second, once in there, we have to influence the direction of the aggressor's behaviour without increasing their resistance. Third, we have to know how to negotiate our safe withdrawal as quickly as possible. This sounds like a tall order but let's see. So we need to:

- engage
- intervene
- withdraw.

The Dysphoric Crisis and The Vacuum

Before we look at these steps in more detail, I'd like to say a little more about the dysphoric crisis. Difficult reactive aggression refers to the rising tensions and emotions within the aggressor before the point where they take over from other restraining forces such as thought, reason, social skills, problem-solving skills, conflict-resolution skills and social values. Before the aggressor reaches this pivotal point they may be able to engage in a tirade of abuse that has either been rehearsed beforehand in previous confrontations or in their imagination. As we saw earlier, however, the expression of anger and hostility beyond a very low level increases rather than decreases their levels of arousal and aggression. Furthermore as the levels of arousal increase, the ability to think, reason, problem-solve and articulate are severely hampered. This results in increasing demands on the aggressor to 'hold it together' while their resources are rapidly diminishing. As the demands overtake their resources to deal with those demands the aggressor may experience a point of critical stress in which they are no longer able to continue the confrontation in this semi-controlled way. It is as if suddenly all the forces guiding them through the confrontation abandon them – they cannot think what to do or say in the next second, and seconds feel like an eternity. This is the state in which other emotions such as embarrassment and humiliation suddenly become overwhelming as the aggressor struggles within their own internal crisis. It is as if they are suddenly all on their own, like an abandoned child with nowhere to turn. This is the dysphoric crisis or as I sometimes have called it, 'the vacuum'. This state is intolerable and unless something is done immediately to reduce the demands on the aggressor, they will 'act out' violently – and the only function of that behaviour may be to 'buy time' – to do something, anything, to avoid entering into a state of panic.

Obviously it would be preferable if we could have used the defusing and de-escalating skills identified in Chapter 3 to prevent this state being reached, but sometimes, as in the case with Donna, this is not always a luxury afforded to us. Once that point arrives, the agenda is clear – we have to fill that 'vacuum' very quickly and in a non-toxic way, otherwise it will be left to the aggressor to fill the vacuum with possibly catastrophic results. I use the term non-toxic because if we physically ingest a toxin our bodies convulse and eject the toxin. Similarly if we fill their vacuum with something psychologically toxic, they will spit it back over us – so we have to be very precise in how we do this. There is another problem, however, and that is that we are made of the same stuff as those who aggress against us. Just as the heat rises and their faculties begin to fail them, so do ours. So at this moment, if we put posturing and machismo to one side, we are both little more than frightened children caught up in a terrifying moment. Note, however, how much of the panic is down to just one little thing – not knowing what to do. If we knew what to do that may not only reduce our own level of panic, but also enable us to get on the front foot and take control. The reason we might be allowed to take control is that the aggressor risks losing face and if our leadership helps them avert that possibility, then they may well follow the line of least resistance (more on this later). Obviously it can be argued that in many cases the aggressor will be more familiar with the dark arts of violence than we as professionals are – in which case the crisis is more ours than theirs. That may be true when we come to consider proactive aggression, but here the behaviour is being driven by emotion and the violent outpourings are largely untutored. This provides us with a significant advantage – if we know what to do!

There are two other points about the dysphoric crisis I'd like to mention before moving on to a closer examination of the rapid reaction skills:

- It is not enough to know how to 'fill the vacuum' safely, but we have to be *able* to do so – and that requires taking control of our own bodies.
- It is often assumed that faced with massive and potentially overwhelming violence we need to come up with an equal or greater opposing force – and this is not necessarily the case.

The latter point would be true if we were in a tug-of-war contest, but we are not. When we reach the dysphoric crisis the behaviour is not difficult to change at all. Poke your tongue out and make a silly face and you will see how easy it is to change! The problem appears to be that it is much easier to tilt the aggression towards more troubled waters than to safer shores. On training courses where the Donna incident is enacted before the group, participants often see the violence that follows as inevitable and there is nothing that the professional could do – and that if they were to try anything, it would more likely go wrong than right. In a sense they are suggesting that the balance is already tilted heavily against us and towards violence. This is of course understandable, but that is not to say that it is true. Clearly the vast majority of highly aggressive situations do not result in violence – they are 'near misses' – although no less terrifying for that. The truth would seem to be that at the dysphoric crisis the crisis is in the balance and that there are at least as many factors that would tilt it away from violence as there are those that would tilt it into violence. Imagine being forced to go on a rollercoaster ride and being told that it is 99 per cent safe, but there is a 1 per cent chance that you will sustain some cuts and bruises – that would be really scary but actually the odds are overwhelmingly in your favour! Understandably we may become preoccupied by the 1 per cent and find it difficult to even think about the other 99 per cent. When we think about the dysphoric crisis the odds are in the balance, 50-50, so that might be even more terrifying. However, the dysphoric crisis is by definition in the balance and a feather on one side of the scales may tip it into violence and a feather on the other side may tip it towards safety. Managing the

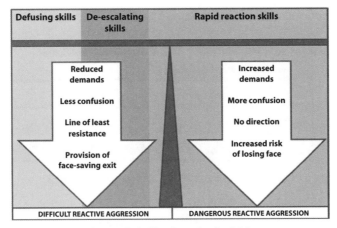

Figure 5.1. The Dysphoric Crisis

dysphoric crisis, therefore, is not about doing big things, but small things that shift the balance and the balance only remains at 50-50 if we leave it to chance. This chapter is about improving those chances, and the skills in tilting the aggression away from violence.

Figure 5.1 shows the dysphoric crisis. As can been seen at lower levels the defusing and de-escalating skills from Chapter 3 reduce the demands and the confusion of the aggressor while providing an easy and face-saving way out for them. As the emotions and levels of arousal increase we get closer to the pivotal point when the behaviour could go either way. Here events can accelerate rapidly and if we are to manage these events we may well have to act faster than we can think – but the goal is still to reduce both the demands on the aggressor and their level of confusion while providing an easy and face-saving way out.

Step One: Engage

The first thing that is apparent is that in situations like the one presented in the case study doing nothing can't be the right answer. Doing nothing left Pat (the professional involved) to be controlled by Donna who was herself completely out of control. Clearly not a good idea. The trouble was that Pat didn't know what to do to take control of herself and Donna. Thinking was too slow, and anything that she could think of seemed more likely to make things worse rather than better. As in Chapter 1, our mantra remains the same – 'do something, not more, less but always something'. But what is that something?

Figure 5.2. The Agenda for Step One – Engage

Let's look at the agenda. As you will see from Figure 5.2, unlike the agendas for the defusing and de-escalating skills where the focus was squarely on managing the aggressor's behaviour, here we have to manage our own behaviour as well. The problem is that it is clearly more desirable for you to influence events than for the aggressor to do so. However, you may have very little idea as to why the aggressor behaves the way they do and it might feel that whatever you do is more likely to be wrong than right. On top of this, even if you are able to think fast enough and come up with a plan of action, by this time your body may already have shut down, gone rigid, started to shake, jolted or whatever – and be unable to respond as you would wish.

Clearly if your body rebels, there is little point in going any further so let's address this first. I am aware that in many cases it will seem as though your body reacts before you have had time to think – especially if you are suddenly taken by surprise. Indeed if our solutions to the problem depend upon thought then we should stop here. However, there remains the question, what triggers off this bodily reaction? As described in Chapter 2 all the signals from your body's sensory receptors – taste, touch, sound, sights, smell, etc. – are initially sent to the thalamus which categorizes these inputs under one of three broad categories, the same way your email program will label incoming emails. In the same way as all the sensory signals are directed to your thalamus it decides, on the basis of past experience, what to pay attention to (e.g. this book), what is not relevant right now (e.g. the sound of a car passing by) but also it should pick out anything that you might have to deal with immediately (e.g. a brick being thrown through your window). It is only when your thalamus has spotted the threat that it activates the limbic system directly without accessing the frontal cortex (the thinking bit) first. Then the signals go directly to the amygdala and on to the hypothalamus, which sends hormonal signals to the adrenal glands, which then release adrenaline and cortisol into the body preparing it for rapid reaction. (Please refer back to Chapter 2 if you need to review this in more detail.)

Two important questions then arise. First, is it possible to recognize that your thalamus has spotted danger before your body reacts? Second, is it possible to influence how your body reacts in response to that recognition? I believe the answer is yes to both questions, but not if you wait for something terrifying to happen and then try to work it out. On a training course it is possible to demonstrate this and participants can check it out for themselves. It's rather more tricky, however, to do this through the written word, but I'll try.

The clue is not in trying to 'think' if you are in danger, but in recognizing how you 'sense' danger. Actually my experience is that people are rather good at this. The focussing response that precedes both the acute stress response and the emergency psychological processes (Chapter 2) corresponds to the point where the thalamus spots danger. It is the point when we experience alarm, or a sudden increase in alertness. For many of us it will be the point where we may let out an involuntary expletive. This refers to a state of hypervigilance, where all the senses open, and is the equivalent of 'Stop, Look and Listen'. It is this moment that it is vital the professional can recognize. For most of us this 'thalamic radar' is immediate, intuitive and accurate. However, if we are survivors of trauma, this thalamic radar may have learned to miscue danger signals. If it was a type 1 trauma (a single overwhelming incident) – for example being attacked in a restaurant – our thalamus may learn that restaurants are dangerous places and our gut feeling about restaurants may be misleading. If it is a type 2 trauma (where the same violation is repeated over a period of time) or a **type 3 trauma** (where many different violations are experienced over a period of time) then our thalamus may begin to see violence as the norm and fail to detect the difference between danger and non-danger. There may also be further complications should we be troubled by psychotic experiences (see Chapter 6) but with these caveats, normally our thalamus is remarkably accurate in sensing danger.

If you can spot or sense the moment when danger enters your world, then so long as you are prepared, there may be a way of taking control of your body, avoiding the acute stress response (flight-fight-freeze), and reacting rapidly and safely. In a fascinating article by Gozzi et al. (2010) scientists at the European Molecular Biology Laboratory were able to switch on or off the freeze response in mice by activating or deactivating specific neurons in the amygdala. So we know that we have at least the time the danger signal takes to get from the thalamus to the amygdala to positively influence the way our body reacts – admittedly it's not a lot! Actually if you look about you, you might notice that people do this more than you would imagine. What does a parent do when they see their young child walking towards the traffic? What do soldiers do when told to charge the enemy? What do martial arts combatants do when in a contest? Or indeed some of our top tennis players? They scream or shout! Now imagine freezing with fear – what do you do? You take a sudden intake of air and your body goes rigid. You might want to experiment yourself a little. Take a sharp intake of air and notice what happens to your body. Now try shouting something out loudly and see how your body reacts. It seems that a scream or shout at the point when aversive stimuli are spotted by our thalamus effectively deactivates the cortex and activates the limbic system thus allowing rapid processing of and reaction to the incoming data – Joseph LeDoux's 'low road'. Now I am not proposing that from now on we should go around screaming ad lib for fear that we might one day freeze – we might not freeze, but our professional credibility might take a battering! It does, however, give us a clue as to where to look in identifying a professional and effective response to immediate danger.

We are now ready to put this all together and identify the rapid reaction skills:

Recognize How You Sense Danger

So the first thing to do is to recognize how you experience the moment that danger enters your world. Reflect on incidents in the past where you have suddenly experienced danger and recognize the immediate sensation in your body. They don't have to be threats of interpersonal violence – maybe you can recall losing your footing and falling down the stairs, or falling asleep while driving and suddenly waking up, or hearing a sudden loud noise. You might get a sudden hot flush, feel prickly, feel something in the pit of your stomach, or zone in and become highly focussed, for example. I think that is well within the capability of most of us.

Identify a Single Syllable Generic Word

Next, identify a single syllable word that you could say aloud the moment you sense you are under threat. One syllable, because anything more increases the demands on you and extra pressure is the last thing you need at this point. It's better to avoid names as sometimes you may not know a person's name, or you may be slowed down by having to recall their name. Swear words and religious references are also best avoided both because they may cause offence and because if the aggressor is in a psychotic state they may be drawn to powerful dichotomies such as God and the Devil, or good and evil. Words like 'sir' or 'madam' can come across as officious and place you in greater danger if they are already raging against the system. Avoid gimmicks like shouting 'fire!' because if the aggressor has a gun they might shoot you, and anyone who may have been able to help will probably be running from the building! Instead 'wait', 'please', 'no', 'hey' might be appropri-ate. It is important that whatever word you choose, you only choose one as having to make a choice between one or more alternatives will activate the frontal cortex which is too slow and may result in panic. Make sure, however, that you are confi-dent about your choice of word for all imaginable emergency scenarios. Personally my choice would be 'Wait!' (maybe I am unconsciously hoping that if they plan to hurt me, 'wait' might subliminally plant the idea that 'later' is an option!) but you should choose the word with which you feel most comfortable.

In the Barclay family story, Pat didn't react fast enough and as an unintended consequence left Donna with the responsibility for filling the vacuum. Pat didn't know what to do but just saying 'wait' might have prevented her body from shut-ting down and taken the pressure off Donna. Saying 'wait', however, can be done in a multitude of ways covering a multitude of meanings. There can be no doubt the tone, volume, physical gesture, facial expression, posture and so on will dra-matically change the nature of the communication. These non-verbal aspects of our behaviour and the associated communications that go with them, however, are not static – unless of course we are doing nothing – and then thinking about them in a crisis is not likely to improve the situation. Let your limbic system take care of your non-verbal communications – the most important thing is that you respond naturally without battling with your body. As long as you just keep to the one word and your intentions are genuinely to resolve the crisis without other agendas, your non-verbal behaviour should be fine.

Keep It Simple

Once you have started with your chosen word, you will need to keep repeating it. This achieves a number of objectives. For you, it removes the pressure to think of what to say while avoiding toxic or triggering statements. At the same time it keeps you on the front foot and takes the pressure off the aggressor who otherwise might fill the vacuum with a dangerous outpouring. It is important that the word is used expressively because it isn't just a 'filler-in' but a personal communica-tion. It doesn't matter at this point whether either of you are able to put that communication into words, but it is important the aggressor can sense that you are acknowledging them and have received the message – whatever that might be. Furthermore, this will convey that you are a sentient human being and not a faceless part of 'the system'. Racists can attack an individual from a minority eth-nic group when they can label them as 'just one of them' and the same is true of homophobes and even football hooligans. Even in domestic violence, a very inti-mate form of violence, often the aggressor will depersonalize their partner before attacking them. 'You (this, that, or the other)!' effectively reduces their partner to 'one of them', and therefore easier to attack. Service users can scream at you when they just think of you as anonymous, but recoil with embarrassment when they realize that you are a feeling, sensing human being.

So this is the first bit, an emotionally and repetitively expressed 'Wait, wait, etc.' and nothing else until we achieve our first set of goals. So what are those goals?

- to stop your body from going into a state of tonic immobility or saying something ill-judged;
- to fill the vacuum – that point between you and the aggressor where neither seems sure of what to do;
- because no demands are being made of the aggressor they may allow you to take up the reins if it lessens the pressure on them;
- to slow them down and interrupt the processing of internal thoughts that could trigger an escalation;
- during this period, which might last for a few seconds up to a minute, physical changes will take place in their body that may require them to re-adjust. Principally their breathing will very likely become faster and shallower and this is likely to lead to an oxygen deficit which may result in having to take an extra breath or 'heave'.

By this point the aggressor may well be on 'the back foot' and become increasingly reliant on you to help them through the crisis without 'losing face'. In addition, the high level of arousal and the repetition of one word induce a dissociative state (see next section) both in us and the aggressor. This is the point where having safely engaged with the aggressor, we move to influence the direction of their actions.

I am often asked, 'What should I do with my hands?' 'Should I return the gaze or not?' 'Should I stand up or remain seated?' 'Should I talk quietly and calmly, or loudly and authoritatively?' – and the list goes on. I believe these questions are false friends and miss the essential point about rapid reaction skills – which is to react before you think. Now I am aware that this is unusual advice as the most basic definition of professional behaviour would be to think before you act. Furthermore, if I am advocating 'action before thought' (only in an immediate crisis, I should add) doesn't that run the risk of behaving unprofessionally? Actually no, because you are not going to make up your mind what to do during the incident – that is far too late. The idea of this chapter is that you will already know what you are going do and those skills are designed to stop you from behaving unprofessionally.

Action Summary: Step One – Engage

1 Learn to recognize the unique experience in your body the moment when danger enters your world.
2 Identify one, and only one, single syllable word (e.g. wait) that you could interject with, without need for thought, the moment you sense danger.
3 Do not attempt to micro-manage your non-verbal behaviours.
4 Continue repeating that word expressively until the aggressor tries to re-adjust.
5 You are now ready to enter into Step Two – Intervene.

Step Two: Intervene

Our task now is not to effect gross changes in the aggressor's behaviour, but to change the direction of that behaviour, or to tilt that behaviour away from danger and towards safety. Clearly, most people don't like the idea of someone controlling their behaviour and so it will be important to effect any changes without the aggressor raising resistance. For this reason I call these '**under-the-radar skills**'. Donna's behaviour feels a bit like a runaway train heading in our direction and it is natural to feel that it would take a superhuman effort to stop it, let alone put it into reverse. An understandable analogy, but one that may mislead us. Both Donna and Pat are on a rollercoaster of emotions that threaten to spill over into uncontrolled violence, but it is important to understand that emotions and behaviour work in very different ways not only to plumbing systems (the catharsis fallacy) but to trains and fairground amusements. The truth is not that Donna's behaviour can't be changed, but rather that it 'feels' as if it could be changed too easily – and for the worse. The wrong look, word or action 'feel' as if they might unleash a torrent of violence – and of course they could. However, this is likely to be an attribution error. We have a tendency to see situations from our unique but egocentric view, and to focus primarily on the things that can go wrong. Yet the truth is that most highly charged, volatile and threatening confrontations do not result in violence. I have been in a number of situations where I feared the worst having seen my life flash before me and yet not one of them ended in an assault on me – they were very near misses. This was not down to sublime skill – I had no idea what I was supposed to do – but pure chance. The odds are not stacked against us, but for us. That doesn't make it any the less terrifying – if you had to put a revolver to your head which had five blank cartridges and one real one the odds would also be in your favour! All I am saying is that if you did a force

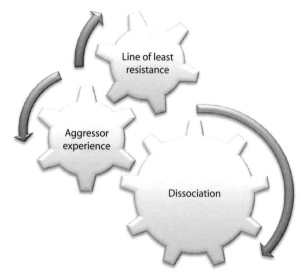

Figure 5.3. Factors Influencing Intervention

field analysis of the moment when Donna pulled the knife on Pat the odds would be against rather than for Pat being cut. The other part of the real story is that although we experience the incident through our own eyes, there are in fact two people in this story. We might think that Donna is on a mission to harm us, but she too is struggling in the dark – as indeed most reactive aggressors are.

Clearly the situation is in the balance and it wouldn't take much to tip the situation one way or the other. We need to find those factors that will tip the situation back in our favour and away from the attack. The factors that I consider important here are:

- the line of least resistance
- the aggressor's experience
- dissociation.

As suggested by Figure 5.3, these factors do not operate in isolation, but interact with one another in such a way that changes in one will result in changes in the others. They are dynamically linked. The level of dissociation will affect the aggressor's second by second experience, which in turn will either open up or close down the line of least resistance. So let's look a bit further.

Dissociation

We dissociate when our brain and our body develop lives of their own and begin to operate independently. For example, in my cheese story, although my frontal cortex was saying, 'Stop it Iain, it's ridiculous, just walk away', my body kept chasing my housemate around the house – thought had no influence on behaviour. When you are asleep you might find that you are caught up in some wild adventurous dream oblivious to the torment you cause your partner with your grunts and random flailings. You can return from work, flop in front of the television and yet when your partner comes in half an hour later and asks what you have been watching, you suddenly realize that you have absolutely no idea. Dissociation kind of gives your brain a rest. Indeed dissociation can be seen as a defence by making terrible things feel unreal. Dissociation can be our friend.

The concept of dissociation is critical to our discussion here because the strategies in the entry stage lead to high levels of dissociation for both us and the aggressor. For both, the high levels of arousal will naturally activate LeDoux's 'low road' and make thought not only difficult but unhelpful. In both cases the need to think would likely result in panic – lots of self-directed questions but no answers. Furthermore, by expressively using a simple repeated word we have taken the pressure off both of us to have to think. For us, this avoids the risk of saying or doing anything that could be inappropriate, toxic or triggering, while for the aggressor it prevents them from revisiting the thoughts that may have led to the sudden and rapid escalation.

This alone would be a significant achievement but there is more. We have also activated the emergency psychological processes identified by Dyregrov et al. (2000) and explored in Chapter 2. In brief, these include the deactivation of emotional reactions, focussed attention, the rapid processing of incoming data and the activation of prior emergency learning. In other words our body becomes our friend and begins to take us through the crisis millisecond by millisecond, processing accurately volumes of information that would overwhelm our frontal cortex. It's interesting to note that hypnotic trances are also dissociative states and these are states of high suggestibility. Now I am not going to suggest for a moment that in the middle of a violent outpouring we are going to hypnotize the aggressor – hypnotic trances are usually induced through relaxation and that is a far cry from how the aggressor will be feeling during an attack. Nonetheless if we take a closer look there are other similarities. Hypnosis, like the peri-traumatic state that we and the aggressor may be in, relies on focussed attention, deactivation of inhibitory thought processes and deactivation of emotional reactions – the emergency psychological processes identified in Chapter 2. Whereas the hypnotherapist may use these states to effect gross behavioural change (e.g. cessation of smoking) our goals are far more modest. All we are looking for is for Donna to take a step back, pause for a moment, or lower the knife. In a fast flowing dynamic crisis this may not seem such a tall order, especially when we consider that the word crisis implies a state of change or a turning point. In fact, in such states small things can result in huge reactions. As stated earlier, when we are asleep and dreaming we are in a dissociative state. It is in this state that most of us will have experienced a myoclonic contraction (aka hypnic jerk) in which a very slight muscular spasm evokes an extreme sensation of falling. That is our goal here – to set the conditions whereby a very small change may induce a huge reaction that pulls Donna back from the brink.

The Aggressor's Experience

We have already identified that during a critical incident our attention becomes highly focussed so when Donna pulls out the knife there is little doubt where that focus will be concentrated. We are very good at 'thin-slicing' the most relevant information in a crisis – and right now it is the position of the knife and everything else is likely to slip into the background. However, we must always remember that there are two people in this crisis and the other is Donna. Her attention is not likely to be focussed on the knife but on whatever poses the greatest and most immediate threat to her – and that happens to be us. Consequently, the knife which looms so large for us, for her recedes into her peripheral vision as she looks straight at us. No doubt Donna will remain acutely aware of the knife in her hand, it's just that she is not looking at it right now. Now if we can induce a sense in her that holding the knife is interfering with the capacity to deal with the interpersonal crisis in front of her, maybe she could be influenced into removing it as an unhelpful distraction.

Physically there are some factors that may also play an important part. The high levels of arousal and the increased body heat will lead to increased perspiration and among other things 'sweaty palms'. This may well affect Donna's grasp of the knife and as she becomes aware of her insecure grip on the knife it is likely that she will attempt to tighten that grip. As she does so, however, this is likely to make the feel of her grip on the knife even more insecure as the muscles in her hand and arm weaken, lose strength and feeling and might even begin to tremble. The chances are, of course, that we won't notice this but she almost certainly will. Staring ahead, dissociated, unable to think or problem-solve and struggling with her grip on the knife, Donna is in crisis – a crisis that can swing either way but which our actions may influence significantly.

Line of Least Resistance

The third principle underpinning the dysphoric crisis is that when people have no time to think and are under huge amounts of pressure to act they are likely to follow whatever route makes life easiest. Left to their own devices we can't know what route they might choose, but if we can offer them a ready-made path through the crisis before the pressure on them to act becomes overwhelming, they might just take it. Of course there are various criteria that this plan must meet. First, we have to present them with it before they embark on a more dangerous plan of their own – and for this reason it has to be ready-made; i.e. we need to have prepared it before we even knew that this situation would arise. Following from that it is obvious that the plan must be generic – that it will fit all circumstances as we will have little or no time to choose between plans as the crisis escalates. Next, whatever it is, it must be immediately do-able and unambiguous – if it is in any way unclear or difficult to carry out, by definition it won't be the line of least resistance and the aggressor will go their own way. For that reason it must be behavioural and involve no more than one act and should feel natural. Finally, the line of least resistance must involve no embarrassment or loss of face otherwise the aggressor will almost certainly kick off again and re-calibrate the crisis until they can find a shameless way through the crisis.

Putting It Together

As soon as the aggressor appears to be re-adjusting, trying to catch up or is looking uncertain we give a single action instruction. This instruction needs to focus on whatever single action is likely to result in the biggest shift in the overall crisis. If there is a weapon, including a fist, that would be the natural focus. Otherwise the space between them and us is where we should concentrate our attention. Obvious commands would be 'put it down', 'drop it', 'step back' and 'back off'. I can appreciate that some readers may feel uncomfortable with issuing direct commands to someone who is already in a highly agitated and reactive state but it is important to recognize that this is already an extremely uncomfortable and dangerous state of affairs. The tone and manner in which you give the commands will obviously greatly affect the way they are received but trying to micro-manage your non-verbal behaviour, as discussed earlier, is unlikely to be helpful. The most important thing is that your attitude is right and then the non-verbal communications will flow naturally from that. What you are trying to communicate while issuing the commands is that:

- they have your undivided attention;
- you are taking them seriously;
- you mean them no harm;
- you want to resolve the situation;
- it will be easier working with you than against you;
- there will be no loss of face for them.

There is no way of knowing whether they will comply with your command immediately, after some repetition, or not at all – but without your direction the demands on them to act in a potentially catastrophic manner, simply to avoid feeling stupid, may increase dramatically. Indeed there is much evidence to suggest that people in crisis look for others to take control and the social psychology literature is filled with studies demonstrating the different effects of leadership, non-leadership and followership.

Once a command is given it is important to repeat it until the aggressor complies or explicitly rejects the command. This is the same as the 'broken record' technique outlined in our discussion of de-escalating skills. As mentioned there, the command should remain the same, without justification, variation or elaboration but should be delivered expressively rather than monotonously (as implied by the term 'broken record'). This narrows the crisis down to one action rather than the complex array of dynamic processes that surround it. In effect the aggressor is being offered a simple route whereby one action could take them away from an overwhelming interpersonal crisis. Furthermore, the repetition increases the likelihood of dissociation and reduces the possibility that the aggressor may be able to access thought processes that might offer alternatives to them. What we are looking for here is not total obedience or a massive or even obvious change in their behaviour, but simply a tilt in the direction away from violence.

If they are wielding a knife and we ask them to put it down we should not expect that they drop it on the floor, simply hope that they lower it slightly. If they do so then the momentum and the direction has changed and we are on track – now is not the time to push for more. The aggressor will have experienced something change even if they don't know what. If they can achieve this, we are ready to move on to the final step.

If they don't at least minimally follow our command three alternative scenarios emerge. The first is that their behaviour continues unchanged. Here we can take advantage of the fact that they are dissociating and the dynamics and physiology of the attack. There is a tactic sometimes used in hypnotherapy called an **implied suggestion**. Of course, the last thing we want to do here is to get clever, but the implied suggestion in this context is very simple. What we want them to do is put down the knife (for example), but it appears that they are resisting our request. However, if we could make them feel that the knife is going down anyway, even though it isn't, they might for a moment believe it is and then drop it to avoid looking stupid or confused! If we tackled this head on by telling them that they are dropping the knife, they may well resist along the lines of 'no it isn't' while raising it. So we have to go under cover and imply that it is dropping without actually saying so and in that way the suggestion is very difficult to reject. So how does this work? Keeping things simple, as always, we continue with the broken record technique but intersperse our commands with the phrase 'that's it' or even 'good', implying that they are already doing what they have been asked to do. They may then become more conscious of the weight of their arms, their tiring muscles, the grip on the knife slipping as the perspiration is released into the palm of their hands. They are still looking at us and not the knife and so it would be difficult to check out whether or not they are dropping the knife. With little or no time to think, they might just drop the knife if only to reduce the source of their confusion, or to show that dropping the knife was their choice not ours! Who knows what the probabilities are, but small things can make big differences.

The second scenario is that our repeated commands aggravate them further and they move closer to us shouting something along the lines of 'don't tell me what to do!' or 'say that one more time and I'll…' Clearly this is not the point to inform them that according to this book you should continue with the broken record technique! Something, however, has changed – they are articulating their demands clearly. In effect they are saying 'don't do that, otherwise I'll have to do this'. It's a kind of deal they are brokering in which they are communicating a desire not to proceed with the attack and telling us what would help here. The simplest response would be to agree with them: 'OK if you want me to stop telling you what to do, I'll stop. I'll do whatever you need of me.' That in itself may be sufficient to result in them stepping back or lowering the weapon – which is the shift or tilt that we have been working towards. Even if they tell us to shut up, we can appear to comply without going immediately mute, 'Okay, if you want me to shut up, I'll shut up. I'll do whatever you think will help.'

The third scenario is that instead of following our commands they make demands of their own. This was the situation with Donna – she started screaming at Pat to 'get up!' Under normal circumstances there could be little room for confusion to occur between two short words – get and up – but these were not normal circumstances. Pat's life depended upon an accurate interpretation – was it an invitation to leave, a challenge, or just random words? Yet if Pat was to get up that would bring her closer to Donna and the knife and it might be misinterpreted as an attack. If, however, Pat didn't get up she would be resisting Donna and her knife and as we saw that led to further violence. Of course, Pat could ask Donna what she means by 'get up' but this is not the time for a discussion or to place demands on Donna to justify herself. Questions can be either easily rebuffed and take us into uncharted territory. Instead there is a third way, which is simply to 'broadcast' our intentions 'Okay, I'll get up. If you want me to get up, that's what I'll do.' In this way we alert the aggressor to our intended actions and so avoid a triggering response and we also give them a chance to confirm or otherwise that

that is indeed what they intended. If they continue to tell us to get up we have little alternative but to do so. We have, however, reduced the risk of misunderstanding their intention or of them misinterpreting our action as anything other than compliance. Of course if they say something along the lines of 'You're going nowhere' at least we have avoided making a very big mistake!

Action Summary: Step Two – Intervene

1 Focus on the most immediate danger which will either be the weapon (if there is one) or the space between you and the aggressor.
2 Use the broken record, repeating expressively and emphatically, a simple one action command – usually 'put it down' or 'step back'. No explanations or elaborations.
3 Implied suggestions (e.g. 'that's it' or 'good') can be incorporated if the broken record isn't sufficient.
4 Broadcast any intentions to act.
5 You are now ready to move on to Step Three.

Step Three – Withdraw

Once the shift or tilt has been achieved the agenda changes significantly. Whatever caused the escalation of reactive aggression to the pivotal point in the first place is unlikely to still be driving the behaviour – even though emotions may remain high. By now the chances are that the aggressor wants the situation to be over just as much as we do – it's just that they may not have a reverse gear. What they need is a way out that doesn't feel like humiliation. However, it is precisely because we have effectively interrupted their thought processes that they may be unable to think of a face-saving way of ending the confrontation and so it is for us to provide one.

Empathy may seem like a strange subject to bring up at this point but actually it may have a critical role in the resolution or otherwise of the crisis and it can be both our saviour and a false friend. To understand we need to untangle two separate but related threads of investigation. The first is the relationship between empathy and violence while the second relate to the processes commonly associated with the Stockholm and Lima syndromes.

The first thing to note is that empathy and violence are very closely related – in fact so closely related that recent research (Moya-Albiol et al. 2010 and widely reported on the internet) has shown that the brain circuits responsible for empathy are for the most part the same as those involved with violence (the frontal cortex, amygdala and other parts of the limbic system). This appears to explain, according to the authors, why: 'Just as our species could be considered the most violent, since we are capable of serial killings, genocide and other atrocities, we are also the most empathetic species, which would seem the other side of the coin' (FECYT 2010). Indeed there is substantial research suggesting 'a strong, positive relationship between empathy and lower rates of interpersonal aggression and a strong positive relationship between empathy and higher rates of compliance' (LeSure-Lester 2000: 153–161). Indeed, a lack of empathy is often reported as a predictor of sexual offending against women and children (Simons et al. 2002). It seems clear then that the more we can get the aggressor to empathize with us, the more inhibitions they will have about attacking us.

The Stockholm Syndrome

The other part of the equation relates to the processes involved in the so-called '**Stockholm syndrome**'. Many of you will be very familiar with this from some of the high publicity stories in the news but I will offer a brief definition before examining it in relation to immediate and ongoing violent incidents. The term was coined following a bank robbery (in Stockholm, naturally) in which two robbers held four employees hostage for five days. Paradoxically, during the ordeal the victims became emotionally attached to their captors and even defended them after they were freed. The term, also often referred to as 'sympathy with the perpetrator' was coined by Bejerot and is frequently referred to in the hostage negotiation literature and the domestic violence literature (to explain why some people stay with their abuser). Of course there are significant differences between domestic violence, hostage negotiations and ongoing violent incidents. The most obvious is that the first two are relatively slow, long processes while our focus is on very fast, short processes. However, although the Stockholm syndrome is usually thought of in terms of long, drawn-out situations, De Fabrique et al. (The FBI Law Enforcement Bulletin/July 2007) tell us:

> Experts have concluded that the intensity, not the length of the incident, combined with a lack of physical abuse more likely will create favorable conditions for the development of the Stockholm syndrome. Apparently, a strong emotional bond develops between persons who share these life-threatening experiences.
>
> De Fabrique et al. (2007)

So that seems to fit with our criteria but whether or not there is a specific and discrete syndrome, or whether that syndrome fits our purposes, the important point is to understand the underpinning affiliative processes and their implications for practice.

The first thing to note is that there is a hidden danger here in developing empathy with the perpetrator during the incident. All logic tells us that if we are trapped in a room with someone waving a knife about, our priority should be to get out – not because we don't care about Donna in this case, but because the best way to help her is for us to stay alive and get her help. Nonetheless, during the 1990s when I was heavily involved in working with staff after serious incidents, I was often taken aback by how often staff would remain in dangerous situations even when they had chances to leave. This wasn't because, like Pat, they were in a state of tonic immobility, but because they felt a strong empathy for their aggressor – 'I couldn't just abandon them…' Even Pat afterwards reported no hostile feelings towards Donna and indeed refused to press any charges against her. On training courses I often tell a modified version of Donna's story and then have it dramatized in close proximity to the training group and the reaction is remarkably similar – a curious mixture of terror, compassion and concern. It is hard to know how often the Stockholm syndrome occurs but I doubt that it is an absolute all-or-nothing concept. According to the FBI's Hostage Barricade Database System of over 4700 incidents only 23 per cent showed signs of the Stockholm syndrome (De Fabrique et al. 2007). There are strong reasons to suggest that the incidence within the context of the helping professionals, however, would be much higher – at least in relation to reactive aggression with known service users. Unlike traditional hostage situations (e.g. bank robberies, hijackings, etc.) the relationship usually pre-dates the onset of the incident and that relationship is usually predicated on some level of empathy existing between professional and service user. In this context it is interesting that on the courses mentioned above, when I give no prior information about Donna, the training groups report significantly fewer Stockholm syndrome features. Furthermore, on those courses where I relate an incident of proactive aggression from a non-service user there is rarely any empathy reported – this time the fear is tinged with hatred and hostility towards the perpetrator. This flies somewhat in the face of what one of the authors, a retired FBI expert, reports in the De Fabrique et al. (2007) article 'for the Stockholm syndrome to occur, the incident must take place between strangers'. Well sometimes we have to disagree!

A psychoanalytic interpretation of the Stockholm syndrome is that in the hostage situation (and effectively, even if only for a short while, Pat was Donna's hostage) the hostage is regressed to a state where their survival is wholly dependent on the hostage-taker, just like the dependency of an infant on their mother.

As De Fabrique et al. (2007) put it 'Victims are overwhelmingly grateful to their captors for giving them life and focus on their acts of kindness, rather than their brutality.' There are many other explanations, but for our discussion it is enough to note that there are important interpersonal processes operating here that could tip the balance between survival or otherwise.

The first problem, for us, has already been mentioned and that is that the helping relationship may cloud the importance of getting out of the situation as quickly as possible – so we need to reinforce here that, right now, that should be the only imperative. The second problem is that it is not immediately clear how having empathy with the perpetrator helps us, when what we really need is for the perpetrator have some empathy for us. This latter condition has sometimes been called the '**Lima syndrome**' after the Japanese Embassy hostage crisis of 1996, when members of a militant movement took hostage hundreds of people attending a party in the official residence of Japan's ambassador to Peru. Within a few days, they set free most of the hostages, including the most valuable ones. Personally, I think that this is just the other side of the same coin. Hostage-takers, perpetrators, helping professionals, members of the public – we are still all of the same species whatever label we attach.

Donna wasn't a cold-blooded killer but someone who was raging at herself and the world, not Pat. The goal, therefore, keeping in mind that our overall aim is simply to get out safely, is to get the aggressor to see us as a human being and not 'just one of them', reduce their sense of isolation and offering them a face-saving way out.

To this end, hostage negotiators will attempt to get the hostage-taker to humanize their captive ('Can you tell Bill that his children love him dearly and are here waiting for him when he gets out?'). Unfortunately, in our case there is very rarely a trained negotiator to do our bidding and the situation is still far too volatile to take such risks on our own behalf. To talk to Donna about our family right now could be catastrophic when we consider that she has just lost hers! Again, the theme that runs throughout this book returns – we should do something, not more, less, but something. We have in fact already started the process by reacting to Donna's crisis in a very human non-verbal way and now we need to consolidate those gains. Clearly we need to move on from Step Two, if only because it would be ludicrous to continue telling Donna to drop the knife if she has already done so! We do, however, need to avoid another vacuum opening up and so we must continue to do something. By now we should be on the front foot and our faculties will probably start functioning again. Direct statements about Donna ('I can see you're really scared ...') may be rebuffed and trigger a new escalation so instead it may be safer and better to concentrate on inclusive language – using words like 'we', 'both', 'us', 'together', 'you and I' – to convey that this is a shared crisis with no winners or losers. At the same time it may help in the humanizing or personalizing process if we use their name and ours as often as possible, without making it sound too contrived. Here it is more difficult to be as prescriptive as earlier because as we move out of the crisis the options broaden considerably. A typical sequence of statements might go something like:

> 'Donna, if you feel half as scared as I do right now you must be absolutely terrified. There's you, Donna and me, Pat in here and we are going have to work something out together. Maybe you don't know what and neither do I but we are going to find that way together. Whatever happens in the future, neither of us can tell but we can choose what happens between us right now. That is our choice and it has nothing to do with anyone else.'

When the moment feels right – and sooner rather than later – we should signal our intention to leave:

> 'Donna, both for you and me, I need to leave now.'

If she allows you, then obviously we should leave, but broadcasting our actions as we go:

> 'Okay Donna, I'm getting up now and I am going to walk to the door.'

If Donna is in your way, she probably isn't aware how big an obstacle she represents, so tell her what you need her to do:

> 'Donna, I need you to move away from the door.'

Obviously if you manage to get out, you need to alert an ambulance, the police and your manager immediately, remaining in the vicinity but not so close that you feel unsafe.

If Donna continues to hold you hostage all you can do is to continue building the relationship between you and buying time. When it feels safe, it might also be helpful to tell Donna that you have missed your next appointment and the police might be looking for you – but you need to exercise considerable judgment here based on your knowledge so far of Donna and how she feels about the current situation. The last thing you want to do is to accelerate her into a further crisis.

Action Summary: Step Three – Withdraw

1 Keep in mind, however much empathy and concern you have for the service user, the only objective is to get out and away. Once that is achieved you will be in a much better position to identify how to help them and activate other services.
2 Build the relationship between the two of you through using 'inclusive language' – sprinkling words like 'we', 'both', 'us', 'together', 'you and I'.
3 Do not allow silences or pauses to develop until the tension has reduced substantially.
4 Once the tension has reduced, maintain the focus on your need to leave.
5 Broadcast your actions as you are leaving.

Finally

There is a problem – and that is how to develop these skills. Life-threatening incidents hopefully are not regular features of your work and so opportunities to practise them are likely to be rare. Nonetheless, there are similarities between the de-escalation skills identified in Chapter 3 and the rapid reaction skills explored here. The differences relate more to the need to manage one's own physiological and emotional responses and the margins for error than the skills themselves. Consequently, becoming more proficient in using de-escalating skills will be a preparation for that moment when rapid reactions skills become necessary as both sets follow the same behavioural trajectory. Furthermore, I have always felt that one of the signs of professional behaviour is to be able to keep things very simple as everything about us becomes increasingly complex. Imagine being in a case conference where passions start rising and different parties are talking over one another. What would be the best response? Probably it would be to use exactly the same skills as identified in Step One; just not necessarily at the same intensity or with the same risks. So in fact we can practise the rapid reaction skills in lower level professional contexts and in that way, when we really need them, they may come more naturally.

Of course, we are not magicians and none of this is guaranteed. These are guidelines, not prescriptions, using the Donna story to illustrate how to keep things simple in a complex and dangerous situation. I hope others will critique the ideas and practices outlined here and that will help us find better and more effective forms of guidance. Nonetheless, there are some really important points to be made here. First, it is better to know what to do than to panic about what to do – even if what you know to do is imperfect. Second, if the aggressor senses that you know what to do at least there is a chance that they will allow you to take the pressure off them. If, on the other hand, they sense you don't know what to do the pressure on them to act will rise exponentially. Third, it is important to do something if only for your own mental health, as feelings of helplessness during traumatic experiences greatly increase the risk of developing PTSD – in fact 'helplessness' is part of the 'traumatic stress' criterion for PTSD (Kubany et al. 2010). This chapter, if nothing else, describes one way of not feeling helpless when faced with potentially overwhelming danger.

Summary

In this chapter we have reviewed the important factors in dealing with reactive aggression when it reaches the pivotal point where the aggression becomes dangerous. We identified three stages – engage, intervene, withdraw – and specific skills to take charge of the crisis. We have emphasized the need to stay active and not to leave the aggressor in a vacuum where they may feel the need to act out. Although most of us will hopefully not have many opportunities to practise these skills, they are on the same behavioural trajectory as the defusing and de-escalating skills, and so the style should feel familiar.

Top Tips
- Listen to your body – it may alert you to danger long before you are able to assess it formally. Make sure you know what it feels like to be faced with danger.
- Identify a single syllable word you can repeat in place of any dialogue and repeat it continuously.

- Never do more than you need to, but make sure you are always doing something.
- Never leave it to the aggressor to decide what to do.
- Allow your body to make decisions about the non-verbal aspects of your behaviour – do not try to micro-manage these.
- Be aware that in Step Three, although you are trying to activate the processes underpinning the Stockholm syndrome to create an empathic relationship between the aggressor and you, there is a danger that these same processes may make it feel more difficult to leave. You should leave as soon as it is safe to do so.

Chapter Six
Skills for Dealing with Disturbed Aggression
Troubled Minds

In this chapter you will:

- work through the second of our 'walk-through case studies' featuring an example of disturbed aggression that takes place in the office
- explore how different types of psychotic disruption influence potentially violent encounters
- identify specific 'psychotic containment skills' to manage disturbed aggression
- consider how race and ethnicity may affect the way we interpret violence

In this chapter we move on from our examination of reactive aggression into situations where very significant psychological disruptions to the aggressor's perception of reality become the overriding concerns. In fact the skills explored in this chapter are not a substitute for the defusing, de-escalation and rapid reaction skills explored earlier, but a supplement and amendment to them. It is extremely unusual for any kind of violence not to be associated with high levels of arousal and so the psychosis containment skills introduced in this chapter have to take that into account. The focus also shifts away from the difficulties we face in managing our own reactions, as that has already been covered, and more onto developing our understanding of how disturbance can drive violent behaviour. In particular we will focus on the influence of psychotic states as this will be a major concern for many professionals. It is commonly accepted that one in four people will experience a mental health problem in any year (Meltzer et al. 1995) and that percentage will be much higher in any helping professional's caseload. The overwhelming majority of that figure will comprise of people with anxiety, stress, depression and related conditions where there is no association with violence. Approximately 2 per cent of the population have a psychotic state (Mangalore and Knapp 2006) and even here the connection with violence is tenuous. Fazel et al. (2009) in their literature review concluded that although there is an increased risk of violence from people with schizophrenia this is almost entirely explained by substance abuse – and that 'the increased risk associated with this co-morbidity is of a similar magnitude to that with individuals with substance abuse alone'. Nonetheless, the interplay between psychosis and violence is highly relevant both because of the complications it adds to the handling of aggressive behaviour and because many professionals feel under skilled in this area.

The walk-through case study that begins the chapter will hopefully bring some focus to our explorations. From there we will consider the various elements that contribute to a psychotic crisis before illustrating how that understanding can inform good practice.

The Walk-Through Case Study: Meet Manny

This occurs within your work setting rather than in someone else's home and raises issues relating to workplace practices which will be picked up later. As with the first case study you can begin here, at the beginning, if you generally have an ongoing working relationship with your service users. If, on the other hand you usually have very little information about your service users before you come in contact with them, you may prefer to skip to the section entitled 'At the scene'. This case study explores skills in working with escalating and perpetrating levels of disturbed aggression. In working through the case study try to place yourself in the position of the staff member, reflecting on your own thoughts, feelings and actions at each stage. Try not to skip ahead because as I have already said, in practice we don't have the benefit of hindsight and certainly not time-travel!

Background

Manny is a man in his mid-50s. Life has dealt him a poor hand. To those that don't know him he is one of 'the invisibles', a lost soul wandering the streets. He has been variously described at different points in his life by professionals as a 'rough sleeper', 'street homeless', a 'problem drinker', and a 'man with chronic mental health issues'. He is also on your caseload. Despite all the assumptions made about him, he currently lives in a flat on the fifth floor of a large tower block on one of the local housing estates. His flat is a health hazard and whatever strengths Manny may have personal hygiene is not among them. This has raised many complaints from other tenants as has his habit of talking loudly (supposedly to himself) throughout the night.

Manny's history is unclear. He is of African Caribbean descent but no one has quite figured out his exact origins. It is believed that he came to England as a very young child with his family. Sometimes he calls himself a 'Mandinka King' but his story changes according to who he is telling it to. He has been diagnosed with schizophrenia and is visited regularly by his community psychiatric nurse (CPN) whose main concern has been to ensure he takes his medication. He doesn't engage well with the mental health services, or for that matter any services. When he moved into his flat about a year ago he was encouraged to attend day centres, colleges, training courses, to develop social and life skills, to look after his flat and to develop a healthy lifestyle. After six months of intense but largely fruitless work those efforts waned.

Over the past three months, however, the complaints about Manny from the other tenants have increased considerably and there has been a lot of pressure to have him moved on. Along with other professionals you have been visiting Manny in search of a solution. Manny, however, is determined that he is not going anywhere – even though he says that some of the other tenants are frightening him. He has been reassured that no one is going to force him to go anywhere but he remains very reluctant to engage around this subject and typically responds to any questions with 'Can I have a cigarette?' On the other hand, he has seemed quite preoccupied by the CPN – who are they, where do they live, are they married, do you know what school they went to, do they have another name? Naturally you declined to answer these questions.

Over the past ten days you have tried visiting Manny on two or three occasions but there has been no response when you have knocked on his door. You spoke to the CPN and the neighbourhood warden but it appears that they haven't seen him either. When you approach his neighbours they simply refuse to talk to you and walk away.

At the Scene

If you are joining at this point all you need to know is that the incident involves a man of African Caribbean origin, in his 50s who you will have seen in the locality before. He is dishevelled, appears to be lost in his own world and may have a serious drink problem and mental health issues. Most people give him a wide berth, but he is not known to be violent.

The incident occurs in the reception area of your local office. Members of the public have direct access at street level to the reception area but not to the offices or interview rooms. In the reception area there are a number of chairs and low tables with magazines on them and it is in this area that any visitors remain while waiting to be seen. There is a receptionist/customer service officer behind a counter who will normally deal with visitors as they come in. There is no screen separating the receptionist from the visitors but there is a panic button underneath the counter which can be pressed in an emergency.

On this particular day you are in the waiting area in front of the reception counter on your way out of the office. There are two visitors in the waiting area; a well-dressed man, probably in his mid-20s, wearing sunglasses; the other an older woman who appears unsteady on her feet. You also notice that the woman on reception is a temp who is covering for a staff absence. Otherwise there is nothing untoward about the situation.

The Incident

In reading through the following account, pause after each paragraph and reflect on what might be going on for you physically and emotionally, what sense you can make of what is happening, and any thoughts you have about what you would do, or how you would be.

Without any warning, the doors to the waiting area swing open and in bundles the man just described (from here on called Manny). His clothes are soaked even though it's a hot sunny day and it's not raining outside. He is wearing a hoody top, joggers and is clutching a tattered shopping bag which appears to have blood on it. You notice that he has an iron bar in his hand and that his eyes are bloodshot and look wild. He is shouting loudly but largely incoherently. The older woman starts screaming and looks terrified. The young man doesn't appear to react at all and just stares at the man as he continues to shout and wave the iron bar about him. The woman on reception duty looks shocked and puts her hands over her face.

> What are your initial reactions? What do think the priorities are and what do you think you might do?

Manny is shouting loudly but incoherently. He is holding the bar threateningly in front of him and telling everyone to get away from him. He makes several lunges towards you and the older woman as if to ward you off. Then he sits down, crumpled, clutching onto the bag and rocking back and forth. His eyes dart about the room. Then he sticks his fingers down his throat and starts convulsing. By now other staff are appearing out of their offices (behind the reception desk) looking on. Some are loudly expressing disgust while others are clearly alarmed. Manny stares directly at you and screams 'What are you looking at?'

> What thoughts do you have about Manny and his behaviour?

He gets to his feet and starts to approach you holding out a hand covered in sick and then vomits over your front. You recoil suddenly. The older woman is now cowering in the corner while the young man continues to look straight at Manny. Your colleagues remain noisily behind the reception desk, many of them looking at you in apparent expectation. Manny withdraws and sits down again, but now there is a look of terror in his eyes as they dart about the room. He is rocking back and forth, making incoherent moaning noises and tugging frantically at his clothes.

> What do you think will happen next?

He starts shouting again and for the first time you begin to make out what he is saying. 'Get them off!', 'Help me, I didn't mean it, they made me!', 'I'm not well, help me!' His knuckles whiten as he holds on to the iron bar while with his other hand he is reaching towards you pleadingly – 'I killed them, I had to kill them, they made me!' Tears run down his face – 'Please don't let them get me!' He is now pulling his hood over his head and covering his face. He puts his unarmed hand over his ear.

> What do you think he means?

The older woman screams, 'Get him away from me! Why isn't anyone doing anything?' Manny swings around but instead of looking at her his eyes fix on the young man. His voice goes into a deep growl and he starts ranting at the young man. For the first time Manny's attention seems fixed rather than wavering, his voice becoming increasingly loud and menacing. 'What are you looking at? Sister of Satan, Son of the Devil, Whore of Hades! Witch . . . Bitch . . . !'

> What do you think you should do? How about the other staff?

The young man leaps up and strides towards Manny. Manny leaps up too and strikes him violently with the iron bar and then again and again as the young man collapses on the floor. Pandemonium breaks out behind the reception desk and it's impossible to hear what anyone is saying. Some staff members rush into the waiting area and try to stop the attack on the young man but get injured in the process. Eventually Manny is restrained and moved to an interview room. Meanwhile other staff are tending to the young man and the injured staff and waiting for the ambulance and the police to arrive. Except they don't arrive, because no one called them – everyone assumed that someone else had done so . . .

Before reading on, it may be helpful to stop for a moment and reflect on the events described above. In particular:

1 What, if anything, could have been done to prevent the obvious deterioration in Manny's condition in the days, weeks and months prior to this incident?
2 How might Manny's behaviour have been managed, moment by moment, during the incident?
3 Do you think the fact that Manny was from a minority ethnic group played any part in this incident?
4 What arrangements could have been put in place beforehand to ensure that staff were better prepared to deal with incidents in the reception area?
5 How might staff have been able to communicate more effectively with one another during the incidents?

What Happened

The Staff Viewpoint

In 'Donna's story' there were warnings that could have been used to withdraw or take evasive action, whereas here there were none. Some preventative work could have been undertaken in the preceding days and weeks, but for the staff in the office the incident started with Manny's explosive entry. At first glance it would be difficult to know whether he was drunk, psychotic or both. Was he dangerous or just very chaotic? Pat, the staff member in whose shoes you were asked to put yourself, had a whole host of unanswered questions spinning around in her head. Furthermore, there was the responsibility for her own safety, the safety of the visitors, the other staff and Manny. Pat was shocked, surprised and confused, pulling away and unsure of what to do. The young man's apparent indifference seemed strange while the woman's screams aggravated the situation. Pat recoiled as Manny approached and was momentarily distracted by the vomit. When Pat looked up again she noticed Manny's tortured look and became aware of his absolute terror. Compassion momentarily took over from fear when Manny began pleading for help – but Manny was still brandishing the iron bar. Pat wondered if Manny might be a war veteran and all the talk about them 'making him do it' and 'killing them' were references to flashbacks. Pat started calling out to him, but within seconds other staff members were shouting over one another, to the young man, the older woman and to Pat. Pandemonium broke out and it became hard to make oneself heard. As Manny started his tirade at the young man, everyone went silent for a moment and then the young man rose up to face Manny. Apparently, the young man felt that the staff didn't know what to do but that as Manny was older, unfit, and badly coordinated he should be able to bundle him out of the office easily enough.

Throughout the incident the woman temping on reception didn't know whether to press the panic alarm or not. She didn't know if it was loud or silent, if it went straight to the police or not, or what reaction it might evoke in Manny, the visitors and the staff. It appears that many people working in the building did not know what it sounded like and there was no clear protocol as to what to do if it were sounded. In the end no one dealt with the situation, chaos reigned and a crisis became a disaster.

Manny's Story

In telling Manny's story, I have to confess that there is a certain amount of speculation involved as it is largely a piece of detective work based on what Manny was able to reveal himself, and the insights of those who worked with him before and after this incident, and the CCTV footage of the incident itself. With those caveats, this is what we believe happened.

Manny wanted to be left alone. He had doggedly fought his battles when he first moved into his flat a year ago and to a large extent he had won. However, as the collective effort to engage him lessened, he spent increasing amounts of time on his own. Slowly he withdrew into his own world and his condition deteriorated. He could still 'put on a show' when the professionals came around, but as soon as they went he would sink back. Neighbours became increasingly intolerant of his outbursts throughout the night and of the growing health hazard. Feeling that the authorities were dragging their feet, they started taking matters into their own hands. We don't know how far this went, but Manny became increasingly frightened to leave his flat.

Manny's lack of engagement was thought to be part of his condition – the negative symptoms of schizophrenia – withdrawal, lack of motivation, loss of interest, blunted affect and so on. In fact Manny was very aware of the perils that faced him and in particular the efforts being made to move him on. When asked what he thought, however, he didn't have the confidence or social skills to assert his wishes and so just followed the easier path 'Have you got a cigarette?'

With his future under threat from all sides his paranoia increased. Why was the CPN so eager for him to move out? Why was the CPN so keen for him to take his medication? Maybe it's the CPN who is orchestrating everything?

It appears that he began believing that the CPN was in league with the neighbours and was poisoning him with the medication. So he stopped taking his medication. I guess the logic would be that if he needs the medication he will feel worse, but if it is poison he will feel better – either way the CPN mustn't know. At first there was no change as he had sufficient medication in his blood stream to keep him going for a while. Then, as the suppressant effects of the medication wore off, he started feeling more alert. This appears to be the point when he started making enquiries about the CPN. However, he now became concerned that the professionals would notice the changes in him and realize that he was not taking the medication. So he hid from them.

It appears that Manny believed that he needed to get all the medication from his body and started to drink (probably very diluted) bleach. The pain would be hard to imagine so he drank copious volumes of alcohol (probably strong cider) to anaesthetize his gut. The acute pain would make it very difficult to concentrate and problem-solve, and as the pain became more chronic he might experience symptoms of delirium. The stress on his system appears then to have triggered psychotic symptoms that had a very different character to those he struggled with on a day-to-day basis. Manny heard voices most days and for much of the day and yet he coped. He would shout back at them, argue with them and assert himself against them – he believed he was a Mandinka King and voices were mere jealous subjects. These voices, however, felt much more powerful and dangerous and he felt fearful and helpless. All we know about what happened next is that he left his flat – drunk, delirious, psychotic and in acute pain – and somehow found his way to the reception area of this office.

Given the amount of pain and disturbance in Manny's condition it is doubtful if, once he had entered the office, he could put together the sequence of events that led him there. All he could be aware of would-be chaos around him. The iron bar appeared to be for defence rather than attack and his screams designed to ward people (real and imagined) off. His darting eyes, angry shouts, the cowering under his hood and attempts to cover his ears suggest that he was hallucinating and that those hallucinations were external and threatening. Despite all of this he still had sufficient awareness to reach out and plead for help.

The change occurred when he focussed on the young man who was sitting quietly among the chaos wearing his sunglasses. Apparently Manny believed that the voices were emanating from this young man and behind the glasses were the eyes of the devil – so when he rose, it was if the devil was coming from him. Manny lashed out violently at 'the devil' and everyone else as they all came to attack him.

General Considerations

Preventative Work with Manny

Other than increasing security at the entrance to the office – and that may not always be desirable – there was little that could have been done to prevent Manny's calamitous entrance. There were, however, many prior indicators that Manny was descending into a crisis and a more proactive approach may have averted that descent. The difficulties that the mental health services were experiencing in engaging Manny should not have been interpreted as him being resistant, but rather that their goals and Manny's were divergent. The mental health services wanted him to attend day centres, seek out education and training, improve his self-care, engage in CBT and take his medication. Manny, however, wanted to be left alone. It seems fairly obvious that the chances of motivating someone to do things that they don't want to are very slim indeed. So maybe that was a point where instead of 'doing more of the same' leading to increasing numbers of professionals feeling exasperated, it might have been better to use that energy to help Manny achieve his goal. At least Manny might not feel so 'ganged up' on.

Whether the increasing complaints were the cause or the result of Manny's deteriorating behaviour we can't know. Either way, this was a situation that demanded more urgent attention from all concerned. Manny's sudden interest in the CPN, or indeed any unexplained change in his behaviour, should also have raised concerns. Naturally we shouldn't discount the possibility that his increased interest may be a positive sign and I would not want to suggest that we should fear change – only that we should consider how it fits into the overall picture. As it turned out, this was the sign that he was no longer taking his medication, and that his paranoia was increasing. I appreciate that sometimes practitioners feel under skilled in exploring mental health issues directly with service users. At this level, however, I think there is little to fear. Most people with a psychotic condition are far more durable than many professionals think and Manny survives much greater threats on a daily basis than any of our clumsy attempts to help. That is not to say that we should become blasé – simply that there is no need to walk on egg-shells. How one goes about this is beyond the scope of this book, but I can recommend an excellent paper, available online, by Bowers et al. (2009) drawing on the experience of expert nurses covering just this – it's well worth a read.

Manny's mysterious disappearance should also have been taken far more seriously. Often people with chaotic lifestyles do drift away and become lost to the system, but Manny had been around and living in his flat for a good while now. Given the hostility of the neighbours it is not inconceivable that they may have done something to him. The police should be involved here at least in order to determine whether or not he is safe and in his flat. It would have been worthwhile checking whether any other professionals (e.g. the street homeless team) had had any contact with Manny. It is too easy to forget about people like Manny.

Managing the Psychotic Crisis

Let's consider the Manny incident in relation to the Instant Aggression Model. Manny was clearly very frightened, confused and upset. Undoubtedly his fear was driving his behaviour and it could be argued that this was an example of reactive aggression. Indeed the defusing, de-escalation and rapid reaction skills identified in the earlier chapters might well reduce his distress and aggression and that would be a whole lot better than doing nothing.

In Donna's story, if we could pull her back from the brink, slow things down, reduce her level of arousal and provide her with a dignified way out, that could be enough. With Manny, however, we could do all that and we would still have a man being controlled by voices, fixed on his own paranoid thoughts, drunk, delirious and in acute pain – and it is this extra layer of disturbance that requires us to look further.

In order for us to be able to do this we need to know a bit more about the nature of acute psychotic states. First, it is not relevant right now what psychiatric label, if any, Manny might be given – that is for another time. What we do need to understand is what, over and above the emotion, might be driving Manny's behaviour and identify ways of containing that in a way that remains consistent with the ideas explored in the earlier chapters.

The psychotic drivers are the hallucinations and the delusions (which will include the paranoia). The research literature doesn't show any clear link between these and violence, even though Link et al. (1998) have suggested that threat/control-override symptoms (T/COs) are significantly associated with violence. These refer

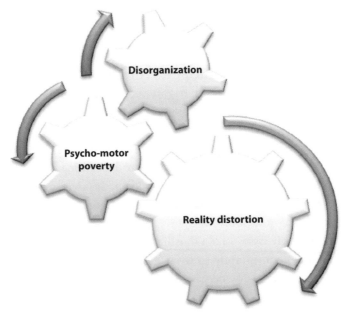

Figure 6.1. Psychotic Disruptions

to, on the one hand feeling overwhelmingly threatened by someone who intends them harm and on the other hand a feeling that their control over their behaviour is being overridden by an external force. However, as already reported more recent research (Fazel and Grann 2006) paints almost the opposite story. Walsh et al. (2002) give a very balanced view. Although schizophrenia is linked with an increase in violence, the vast majority of schizophrenics aren't violent at all and it's very much more likely that if you are going to be attacked it will be by someone without schizophrenia. However, our task is not to predict the risk of violence associated with psychotic experiences, but to identify skills to manage behaviour when that behaviour is already being influenced by psychosis.

The three main types of psychotic disruptions (see Figure 6.1) are:

- disorganization
- psycho-motor poverty
- reality distortion.

Disorganization

Disorganization refers mostly to:

- 'incongruity of affect';
- 'speech disorder'.

Incongruity of affect refers to emotional responses that don't appear to fit the prevailing circumstances – so the person might laugh at something sad, cry at something joyful. This is not to be confused with 'tears of joy' or 'laughing hysterically' in the face of tragedy. Often in very frightening situations people will laugh uncontrollably, but they are still frightened. When we talk of 'incongruity of affect' the person may actually feel happiness in a tragedy, almost as if their emotions have been hard-wired the wrong way round in the brain.

Speech disorder is often referred to as **'word salad'** – ongoing disjointed or rambling monologues in which a person seems to be talking to himself/herself or imagined people or voices. Another aspect is alogia, or poverty of speech and lack of fluency, thought to reflect slowing or blocked thoughts, and often manifested as short, empty replies to questions.

In Manny's case there were no obvious signs of 'incongruity of affect' – his terror was real and related appropriately to what he believed to be happening to him – although there were signs of speech disorder. These levels of disorganization, while highlighting the difficulties in communicating effectively with someone in a psychotic state, do not provide much guidance as to how to manage that state – only that opportunities to use reason are likely to be limited.

Psycho-motor Poverty

These features are often referred to as 'negative symptoms' and include:

- withdrawal
- loss of motivation
- catatonia
- **passivity experiences.**

In Manny's case there were signs of withdrawal and loss of motivation in the weeks and months leading up to this crisis, but certainly not during it – if only! Catatonia is a motor condition associated with stupor in which the person may not move at all, or engage in constant repetitive moments such as rocking. Although Manny did rock back and forth at one stage, this wasn't catatonia but the regressive and comforting movements of a frightened child.

Finally we have passivity experiences in which the person experiences their body being controlled by some external force. The clue to these strange experiences may actually be in the material we have been looking at in the earlier chapters – dissociation and Le Doux's 'low road'. Often after a crisis people will say things like 'I don't know what came over me', or 'It was like I wasn't there, but looking in on myself'. The limbic system takes over from the frontal cortex which becomes a bystander in a crisis. Actually, this does give some clue as to what we need to do. If the person in the psychotic state feels that their movements are being controlled by some outside force, maybe we could become that outside force?

Reality Distortion

These are the major and most relevant disruptions that will be driving the crisis. They are also the aspects of the crisis that many professionals find the most puzzling, impenetrable and disturbing. Paradoxically, as we will see, they may also offer some hope of containing the crisis. So let's look at these in turn before identifying the 'psychosis containment skills'.

The major reality distortions include:

- delusions (including paranoia)
- **thought insertion**
- **thought withdrawal**
- **thought broadcasting**
- hallucinations.

The first four are cognitive processes while the last, the hallucinations, are perceptual processes. Nonetheless, perception and cognition are inextricably linked because if, for example, we believe that we are being persecuted (cognition), hearing a noise outside our door will take on a very different character than if we heard the same noise while waiting for our friends to turn up. For the time being, however, we will consider them separately before putting them back together again.

Delusions

Delusions are usually defined as strong beliefs held despite overwhelming evidence to the contrary. Of course such a definition quickly runs into difficulties – you, for example, may believe in the Hindu God Ganesh, but the fact that most people do not neither invalidates that belief or makes it a delusion. I don't intend to jump into those murky waters here but if you want to explore this further you may want to read an article by David (1999) 'On the impossibility of defining delusions'. Each of us constructs a unique world to inhabit, and your world will be different from mine in as much as we make different assumptions about ourselves, others and the world. For our purposes it is sufficient to know that Manny's experience of the world was distinctly different from those of the other people in the office. The content of that world is something we may never know and it is this 'not knowingness' that can easily undermine professionals. Nonetheless, in a crisis, I would argue that we don't need to know what he believes is happening – it is enough to know that it is causing him great distress.

Thought Insertion, Thought Withdrawal and Thought Broadcasting

These refer to mechanisms whereby someone merges their experience with those of others around them. It is as if only the finest of films separate them from others and that others have far greater control over them than in fact they do. The risk is that if they believe that the others are controlling them they may 'act out' to stop this. These are mechanisms that have to be managed during the crisis. Thought insertion refers to the belief that their thoughts are not their own, but are being inserted by others. So if they have a 'bad' thought, they may believe that they can stop the thought by stopping the person who gave it to them. Thought withdrawal relates to an experience which many of us, perhaps as we get older, experience increasingly – forgetfulness. Sometimes I am in full flow when my mind suddenly goes blank and I haven't a clue what I was about to say – even though I have said it a thousand times before. It is as if all thoughts and memories are suddenly snatched from me. It's not that I have lost the memory, simply I can't quite retrieve it right now and it's my failing. However, with thought withdrawal it is as if someone else took that thought and this could make the person feel manipulated. Thought broadcasting refers to the belief that one's thoughts are being broadcast – that is, as the person thinks something, others are able to hear it. The implication here is that if they believe you know what they are thinking they may feel very exposed and threatened.

Hallucinations

As with delusions there are some complications in finding an adequate definition and again this is not a debate I intend to enter. For our purposes they are sensory perceptions, mostly visual, tactile or auditory that feel real, vivid and substantial, that are not shared by others and appear to have no external origin. These are often seen as the hallmark of psychotic conditions such as schizophrenia although it is possible to hallucinate:

- when in extreme pain;
- when delirious;
- during bereavement;
- under the influence of drugs (prescribed and otherwise);
- under conditions of sensory deprivation;
- as spiritual or religious experiences.

The indications are that it is not the hallucinations themselves that are danger-ous or disturbing, but the relationship the person has with them. If you would like to explore this further there is an interesting article available online by Perez-Alvarez et al. (2008). Many people hear voices, for example, but see them as 'spir-itual guides' or 'providing important insights' or even 'companionship' and don't become unwell. It is when the relationship with voices is negative that people talk of psychiatric conditions.

There are as many different types of hallucination as there are senses, but gen-erally the three that are most likely to be associated with dangerous behaviour are the tactile, visual and auditory hallucinations (touch, sight and sound).

Tactile hallucinations   The most common form of tactile hallucination involves a feeling of insects crawling on or underneath the skin and is mostly associated with (Berrios 1982):

- drug misuse, in particular prolonged misuse of cocaine or amphetamine;
- from the withdrawal from alcohol or benzodiazepines;
- prolonged illness;
- skin cancer;
- hormonal changes;
- high fevers.

These are not in themselves particularly associated with violence, but if you imag-ine insects crawling all over you, you can imagine the effect it will have on your behaviour. Panic, terror, a loss of focus on the events about you, an inability to think or problem-solve, flailing arms and legs, screams, might all enter the mix.

Visual hallucinations   These tend to result from drug and alcohol misuse as well as other forms of poisoning, but are also frequently seen in the later stages of demen-tia when the visual cortex may become diseased. People suffering from dementia can often be seen reaching out and trying to grab things which obviously they can see but are not there. In that case, there would be no danger to others, except that the frustration might lead to outbursts of anger. Visual hallucinations are usually manifested in one of two forms, which I have called:

- the woozy form, and
- the phantom form.

– although I doubt either term will enter into the wider literature! The woozy form relates to a highly dissociated state in which the person appears 'spaced out' and transfixed on the visual hallucinations – this state is not usually associated with imminent interpersonal danger. The other form, the phantom form, is often characterized as a spirit, ghost or demon coming at the individual and the natural reaction is to recoil or take up a defensive stance. Again this is not obviously associated with interpersonal danger, however terrifying these experiences may be.

Auditory hallucinations   While tactile and visual hallucinations are not particularly associated with schizophrenia, auditory hallucinations or voices are. Furthermore as we have seen the tactile and visual hallucinations are not closely associated with interpersonal danger, and any increased risk comes from the fear, panic or confusion that they may stir up rather than the hallucinations themselves. Auditory hallucinations, however, have a different and potentially dangerous quality in as much as they can:

- threaten
- command
- persecute
- badger
- bait
- bully.

The media stereotype of the wide-eyed, cackling, criminally insane monster communicating happily with their voices is a long way from the truth – here we are talking about tormented souls and a better analogy would be the child in the school playground surrounded by bullies. The problem with bullies is that it often feels easier to appease them than confront them – to do as they say rather than risk angering them further.

From the point of view of imminent interpersonal danger during an acute psychotic crisis this is the first place to be concerned because while delusions may fuel the crisis, the voices may be the spark that ignites it – so let's at least keep the sparks at bay. To understand how this might be achieved we need to understand a bit more about how the auditory hallucinations operate. Broadly speaking there are two main types of theory about auditory hallucinations:

- One proposes that the hallucinations result from an inability to distinguish internal processes such as our own internal dialogue from external processes (Frith 1992).
- The other is that they result from a misinterpretation of external events (e.g. Hemsley 1993).

Actually, it isn't clear to me why both can't be true - that each theory applies to a different kind of auditory hallucination. Simply observing people who are hearing voices suggests that they are not all experiencing those voices in the same way. One person may be involved in a continuous, almost sub-vocal dialogue, head down and caught up exclusively in their own world, while another will be shouting out at all around them as if the voices were 'out there' somewhere. Of course it is also possible for one person to experience both types of auditory hallucination.

Our interest is in dangerous behaviour, so let's look at this again. To simplify matters, voices can have either

- an internal locus of control depending on whether the hearer experiences the voices 'in their head';
- an external locus of control where the voices are heard as coming from outside.

By and large, voices with an internal locus of control are more likely to result in personal torment while those with an external locus of control are more likely to lead to a struggle with their environment. Nonetheless, a voice that orders the hearer to attack will be dangerous regardless of whether its origin is experienced as internal or external. However, if the struggler is trying to resist that voice and its origin is believed to be outside of them, then that is more likely to 'act out' rather than 'act in'. When the voices have an internal locus of control we might be able to divert the hearer from their tormenting voices, but when the locus of control is external this is more unpredictable as we are part of that external world.

Hallucinations and the Brain

Returning to our understanding of the brain we can see how this might work. We already know that the thalamus filters incoming sensory signals and ascribes them as, according to our analogy, real mail, junk mail and emergency mail. The question then arises, what happens if the thalamus mis-filters the incoming signals and sends junk mail up to the frontal cortex by mistake? You can try it out – when it's safe and you've got some spare time look at the clouds, or if you are fortunate to live in sunnier climes, lie back, close your eyes and focus on your visual experience. You may well start seeing 'things' in the junk mail because this is now being sent to your frontal cortex which has the job of making sense of the data it receives. I have no idea what you will see and I doubt that it has any Freudian significance, but it might reveal something about your current preoccupations. In the same way the hearer may focus on traffic noise, the wind blowing outside, creaky floor boards, electrical items, even the gurgling in their gut, the wheeziness in their chest or the sound of air through their nasal tract. These signals may have no real meaning, but when focussed on and sent to their frontal cortex they may begin to hear voices in those sounds. The significance of this will be seen when we look at the psychosis containment skills.

If this theory is correct as has been proposed (see Behrendt 2006) there is another factor that we need to take into consideration and that is that the thalamus may not only mis-filter incoming sensory signals, but it may not filter out enough. If someone pulled a knife on you, I imagine that your attention would become very focussed on that knife, pretty much to the exclusion of everything else. In other words, in a crisis your thalamus is doing a very good filtering job. However, this is not generally what we see when people are in acute psychotic states. In those states it often seems like their attention is all over the place – they are highly distracted, hardly focussing on one thing before something else intrudes. Again, this has very significant implications for practice.

Confusion

It is in this overwhelmed state that the hearer might have a **catastrophic reaction** – more normally associated with dementia and learning difficulties – an extreme emotional and physical reaction to events, real or perceived, with which they cannot cope. Confusion, or the inability to understand what is going on around you, can also lead to catastrophic reactions. Confusion can lead to a state of panic in any of us. I might be walking down the street minding my own business when I suddenly see someone approaching me. I try to snap out of my reverie but although I am sure I know this person, right now I can't figure out how they fit into my life. I start panicking as we move ever closer with time rapidly closing down – who are they? Are they a colleague, someone from the gym, a service user, a friend of my partner, someone I met on a course? I just can't think fast enough and as the moment arrives I find myself blabbering inarticulately to my acquaintance – only to discover that she is Tina the checkout assistant from Tescos! I have done no more than grunt at her for the past five years and now I am publicly embarrassing myself before her. Well it's not quite the same order of confusion that we are talking about here, but it illustrates how confusion can escalate a perfectly ordinary encounter into a crisis. If only Tina had been wearing her Tescos uniform . . .

Nicotine and Schizophrenia

Anyone who has worked in mental health will be aware how smoking and conditions like schizophrenia go hand in hand. De Leon and Diaz (2005) have shown that the rate of smoking among schizophrenia patients is up to fourfold of that found in the general population. My own experience also suggests that as people with schizophrenia become more unwell they become even more desperate to smoke. This has led researchers to question whether the nicotine in the cigarettes is providing a form of self-medication. Research in this area abounds but I will just draw your attention to an authoritative review of the evidence by Kumari and Potsma (2005: 1029) which can be viewed online. To quote from that paper:

> To conclude, there is considerable empirical support for the idea that smoking in schizophrenia may represent an attempt to self-medicate some of the cognitive deficits of this disorder. Proposed are a wide range of beneficial effects of nicotine which are explained in terms of the drugs' interaction with dopaminergic as well as glutamatergic transmitter systems. Given that cigarette smoking lends itself to titration to achieve specific pharmacological effects, it is possible that individual patients may use different dosing strategies to achieve such effects.

So why am I referring to this? Well, if we are to have any chance of safely containing an acute psychotic episode, then we need all the tools at our disposal – and if Manny was given a choice between Clozapine and a cigarette, I am pretty sure I know which he would take!

Psychosis Containment Skills

Now that we have explored what we are dealing with we can begin to identify good practice in relation to containing dangerous disturbed behaviour.

Some Important Preliminary Points

Before going further, however, I would like us to be very clear about what we are talking about and what we are not. What we are not talking about is the ongoing work with people who are troubled by psychotic experiences. What we are talking about are skills appropriate for responding to people whose behaviour is becoming increasingly dangerous by virtue of their psychosis. Allied to that, if it is possible to remove bystanders and keep the service user safe while withdrawing to alert the emergency services, then that is obviously what we should do. The skills identified here are for those situations where that is not possible – there may be no way out, other vulnerable people could be present or it may happen too fast.

People don't suddenly become psychotic, it takes time for the psychosis to take over – sometimes this occurs slowly and insidiously over weeks and months, sometimes it may be only days, but it is never immediate. Even if the psychosis is triggered by drug misuse, we are talking about hours. The reason I mention this is that if the service user is a resident in a hostel, or a hospital in-patient, staff should have been aware of their deteriorating condition and taken action long before it reaches the psychotic crisis. If the service user is encountered on a home visit, hopefully by following the recommendations in Chapter 8 a door-step assessment might have led to a tactical withdrawal. Prevention is always preferable.

So really we are talking about incidents that suddenly descend upon us without those preventative opportunities being present – like the example in the reception area with Manny. Indeed this sudden change of scene that gives us our first clue. The moment Manny bursts into the office, it is not just a total shock for everyone present, but for Manny too. Although in a psychotic state, he still has to make sense of where he is, who these people are, and what they are up to and it is this brief interlude that gives us a chance to intervene effectively and get in front of the psychotic material.

As intimated earlier delusions are relatively slow cognitive processes while hallucinations, particularly auditory ones, can be instant. Given Manny's level of distress it is fairly obvious that if he is hearing voices, these are unlikely to be offering him friendly guidance, so our first task (assuming that someone else is removing the onlookers) is to gain his attention and take it away from the voices.

Step One: Gain their Attention

It is self-evident that we cannot influence Manny's behaviour if we don't have his attention. Nonetheless, on my travels I have come across many professionals who act as if people in acute psychotic states are either deaf or unreachable, or that the auditory hallucinations are so loud that they wouldn't hear anything that others had to say. In my view, unless there is a sensory impairment quite separate from the psychosis, none of this is generally true. Many contemporary approaches to working with schizophrenia propose that the hearer often gives far too much power to their voices – and it seems that professionals can be guilty of this too. If we follow our earlier analysis, the voices are likely to emanate either from ambient sounds in the environment or be confused with the hearer's own internal dialogue. Clearly if the hearer is left to their own devices they will have nothing to listen to but the voices and that may not be helpful right now.

So the first thing we should do is to speak, and sooner rather than later. The chances are that we will have to do this quite loudly, not shouting or aggressively, but loud enough to command their attention. As always, it is best to keep this simple. If we know their name, then calling that out would be very helpful as it might help orient them a little.

Otherwise:

- 'Hello'
- 'Excuse me'
- 'Can I have your attention?'
- or if they are threatening to attack, 'Wait!' as suggested with the rapid reaction skills.

Speaking loudly and continuously will not only help them focus on us, but it will also make it more difficult to focus on what the voices might be saying. Again, we should allow our attitude to guide our tone and other aspects of our non-verbal behaviour – provided, of course, that we have a genuine desire to help them and resolve the immediate crisis. There are, however, some two additional considerations here, over and above the rapid reaction skills. These concern eye contact and the use of physical gestures.

When things are happening fast there may be no time to reflect on how much eye contact to have and what kind of eye contact that should be. In any case there are usually far too many factors involved to calibrate this accurately and effectively. However, strange though it might sound, when dealing with psychotic behaviour we might actually be 'more in the know' than in the general case – and there are compelling reasons here why it is better to avoid any prolonged eye contact. I am not suggesting that we should look away which might come across as being disinterested or ignorant, but instead to look at their body rather than their eyes, so that you continue to show interest but without intensifying the psychological interaction.

The reason for this is threefold:

- If they are paranoid looking straight at them is likely to increase those feelings of being looked at and persecuted.
- If they are battling with their own thoughts they may believe that anyone looking directly at them may be inserting, withdrawing or receiving broadcasts of those thoughts.
- The last thing we want to do is to intensify the interactions between them and us, or to make them feel threatened or under pressure.

It is important to remember that frightening as this may be for us, many people troubled by psychotic experiences lack confidence and find social interactions extremely difficult at the best of times.

The point about physical gestures is not about what kind of gestures but how much. Because the person in the psychotic state may be finding it extremely difficult to focus on any one thing, it obviously makes sense not to give them too many different things to focus on. For this reason expansive gestures may be unhelpful. For most of us, these gestures might be interpreted effortlessly and reinforce or emphasize the vocal communication. For someone in a psychotic state, however, they might be struggling hard to work out what we are saying and whether to trust it and then become confused by our gestures. In effect we are running the risk of overloading them and triggering a catastrophic reaction. Obviously this flies in the face of the recommendations in working with people with learning disabilities and people suffering from dementia. In those cases the service user may struggle with speech and consequently hand gestures can be very helpful in aiding the communication without embarrassing the service user. Aphasia, however, is not particularly associated with psychosis – so it's best to use your voice to communicate while keeping the number of sensory inputs to a minimum.

> **Action Summary: Step One - gain their attention**
> 1 Remove onlookers and any other possible sources of distraction.
> 2 Gain the service user's attention by talking loudly to them, but without shouting.
> 3 Continue talking throughout to help take their focus away from any auditory hallucinations.
> 4 Avoid prolonged eye contact as these may be experienced as intrusive and increase feelings of paranoia. It may be better to focus on their body rather than their face.
> 5 Avoid expansive gestures as these may be experienced as threatening and confusing.

Step Two: Provide Reality Checks

Once we have gained the service user's attention, the next task is to ground them and increase their trust in us. In my experience, however major the crisis, it is very rare for someone to be wholly submerged in their psychosis – rather they tend to flit in and out, constantly struggling with what to believe and enmeshed in a confusion of worlds. It is not like they are on Mars and we are still on planet Earth. Manny, just like everyone else in that office saw the door, the chairs, the two visitors, the receptionist, the counter and all the people congregating behind it. The trouble was he didn't know what to trust and which were tricks of the mind.

Our task is to help the service user feel more grounded and confident in their environment and more trusting of us. It might be very tempting to use lots of reassuring words here but in my opinion it is best to keep it very simple. Statements like, 'We want help you', 'No one will harm you' and 'You are safe with us' might sound reassuring but may be received with suspicion and viewed as tricks. Furthermore we are asking him to relate to rather abstract, elusive and intangible concepts. Again this is an example of 'doing more rather than less' and it may be preferable at this early stage to keep things very simple.

If the person is struggling with what to trust, clearly it would be a good idea if we can get them to trust us. First if we follow the lesson from the story about my calamitous encounter with the checkout assistant, we should remove sources of possible confusion and as soon as we have gained their attention, tell them our name, our role and where we are. So if it was Pat dealing with Manny, it would go:

> 'Manny (if you know his name), my name is Pat, I am a (social worker, staff member, etc.) and we're in (the health clinic, housing department, etc.).'

This will minimize the risk of them projecting any of their psychotic material onto us, and reduce the amount of information they have to process. It will also provide a safe way to gauge their response and state of mind.

The next grounding task is to provide information that can be validated. It can be a very scary world when you don't know what to trust and so if we can refer to things that can be seen and possibly touched then they have a way of checking that they are not being tricked:

> 'Manny, you have just come through the door, you are holding onto a chair and those people, the man and the woman, are leaving us . . .'

Because he can see what we are talking about and additionally feel the chair he may gain greater confidence in his environment and in us. By continuing to talk, we keep the focus off the voices and the other people in the office – and furthermore signal to those other people that the situation is being dealt with and there is no need for them to intervene.

> **Action Summary: Step Two – provide reality checks**
> 1 Tell the service user your name, your role and your location – even if you are well known to them – 'My name is Pat, I am a nurse and we are in the lounge'.
> 2 Provide them with information that they can validate immediately. The easiest way to do this is to describe the physical surroundings: 'You are holding onto the door, I am standing behind this chair and the people behind me are leaving the room'.

Step Three: Direct their Behaviour

It is sometimes assumed that because of the chaos, the voices, the paranoia and the extreme emotions involved that people in florid psychotic states will be very difficult to influence. Indeed, why should they follow us when there are so many other distractions, disruptions and diversions? Of course if we just stand back and watch as the spectacle unfolds before us, as happened in the Manny incident, then who knows which of all the competing influences will determine the outcome. However, in the previous two phases we have been narrowing Manny's world down and keeping his focus on us, and in that case if anyone will be able to influence the course of events, it will be us.

The point about Manny's behaviour is not that it is highly resistant to outside influence, but that it is being influenced far too easily. Imagine I come into your office and tell you to (for example) 'Sit down!' My guess is that you probably wouldn't – you might be shocked, surprised, confused, indignant – but you probably wouldn't sit down. How dare I come in and start bossing you about? Manny is no different most of the time. Each day he would hear voices telling him what to do, but he would shout back at them, tell them to leave him alone – in short he would resist them like you would resist my commands. Now consider the same scenario as I walk into the office, but this time you are in a state of absolute terror and I am wearing a police uniform. Now my guess is that you would follow my orders and this is the scenario that we are in. Manny is in abject terror and we have figuratively put on the police uniform by taking control.

Additionally, a major concern is that if Manny is hearing **command hallucinations**, in this state he might actually act on them – that is he might be influenced too easily. The command hallucinations are like bullies and Manny won't obey them because he wants to, but because he is too frightened not to. These voices, however, as we saw earlier are likely either to have their origin in his own internal speech, or come from applying meaning to ambient sounds in the environment. Our voice, however, can be far louder and more powerful than voices coming from either of those sources and so we should use it to positively direct Manny's behaviour.

So as soon as we have gained his attention and grounded him we need to start giving very simple and clear behavioural directions. These might be, 'Manny, sit down', or 'Manny, put the bar down' with the volume, intensity and tone matching the level of urgency. So if Manny is quiet, frightened and looking at us we might talk quietly, although still loud enough to be heard above all other sounds. If Manny is about to assault the young man, we would need to shout. Interestingly this is a case where our voice is more powerful than our fists. The voice is immediate and can halt behaviour in an instant. In contrast a physical intervention takes time, places us in greater danger, might actually precipitate the attack and could increase the amount of force Manny uses to compensate for the force that we have added. It may well be that a shout is sufficient, given the suggestibility indicated by his state of mind, but if not, the broken record technique provides a safe way to continue.

Action Summary: Step Three – direct their behaviour
1 If they have a weapon or their behaviour becomes very threatening, simply tell them in a friendly but commanding way what you want them to do.
2 Be very specific about the behaviour. So instead of 'Stop doing that' we might say 'Please put that iron bar on the table'.
3 If they don't comply, use the broken record technique as described in the earlier chapters.

Step Four: Provide Containment

If we can hold onto the situation long enough to remove bystanders, isolate Manny and keep him safe then our job is done. Away from the crowd Manny should feel much safer and our only task now is to keep it that way until support arrives. Now is the time to

- learn his name, if we don't already know it;
- use his name whenever possible;
- talk in terms of 'we' and 'us' rather than 'you' and 'I' to reduce his paranoia and sense of isolation;
- allow him to talk as long as he is not becoming more agitated.

Non-directive listening skills would be helpful, concentrating on reflecting back the feelings rather than the content. So for example, if he refers to the psychotic content – 'They're all around, they're going to get me' – rather than trying to challenge or explore this further, we can just say 'That must be very frightening, but no one will hurt you'. All that matters is keeping the situation safe. If he is a smoker offering him a cigarette may help – regardless of rules about smoking in public places! It may give him a break from the hallucinations and delusions and convey that we understand and can meet his needs. As a non-smoker, I don't carry cigarettes with me, but it is still possible to use the offer 'Come with me, and we will get some cigarettes' or 'I'm going to see if anyone has got some cigarettes to give you.'

In Manny's case, when help arrives it is certain that he will need to go into hospital – both for his physical and mental health issues to be assessed and treated. If possible it would be helpful to accompany him in the ambulance to provide him with reassurance and to ensure that he has an advocate at the hospital.

Race, Mental Health and Violence

So far I have not commented on the racial, cultural or ethnic aspects of this incident because I would hope that we would apply the same principles and practices to contain the acute psychotic crisis regardless of who is involved. We have to accept, however, that we all have prejudices, even where we believe that we may not. I think I am staunchly anti-racist and would be feel mortified if anyone were to suggest otherwise. However, we are often unaware of our biases and even though they may be unconscious, they are still present. If you have any doubts about this you might try the Harvard **Implicit Association Test** for Race – there are others for gender, sexuality, religion, weight, age, disability – even weapons and presidents. Unlike psychometric tests, you can't cheat and the results are sobering – or at least they were for me. You can find the link to these at www.facingdanger.com.

It is undeniably true that people are discriminated against both because of their race and their mental health issues – and that when these combine, the stereotypes multiply rather than add up. I can't comment on what implicit associations the people in the office made when they saw Manny enter, but my guess is that for the most part they weren't in his favour - and obviously these aren't factors that could be taken into account during the incident. On the other hand who knows what the cumulative effect over the years of those biases on Manny might have been. Clearly a fairer society would be a less violent one.

Mind, the mental health charity (www.mind.org.uk) has some very helpful fact sheets in relation to both race and mental health and dangerousness and mental health which you may wish to explore. Here I would just like to draw attention to a couple of points. Studies show that the rate of diagnosis of schizophrenia is between two and eight times higher within the African Caribbean community (in the UK) when compared to that within the white population (Harrison 2002). Some of that alarming statistic might be down to the cumulative effect of discrimination, oppression and the higher levels of unemployment, poverty and family breakdown that follow as a result. At least at that level we can be righteously indignant at the failures of our society and political leaders.

More worryingly, however, Nazroo and King (2002) tell us that research suggests that despite their being no research evidence that African Caribbean people are more likely to be aggressive than their white counter parts:

- staff in mental health hospitals are more likely to perceive them as potentially dangerous;
- psychiatrists are more likely to consider this group as potentially dangerous to others;
- African Caribbean people are more likely to be diagnosed with psychosis because of bias among those who treat them.

I guess that means that we may be part of the problem.

Summary

In this chapter we have looked at how various psychotic experiences add to the difficulty of managing aggressive behaviour and have considered various skills aimed at managing the different disturbances found. The defusing and de-escalation skills remain valid for dealing with people in highly disturbed states, so these psychosis containment skills are essentially supplementary to those.

Top Tips
- If you have little or no experience of working with people in acute psychotic states, the best way to treat them is just how you would treat anyone else.
- People in acute psychotic states are not in entirely separate worlds - they see and hear what is going on around them just as you do. They may, however, not be sure what they can trust and may have addition perceptual experiences (e.g. hallucinations). The primary task is to increase their

sense of trust and safety while making it more difficult for the psychotic experiences to intrude.

- The skills for dealing with people in acute psychotic states are not complex, but it helps to know them. Just the fact that the service user senses that you know what you are doing may be enough to make them feel sufficiently safe to follow you.
- We all have biases and we will never get rid of them, but it helps to know what yours are and how to deal with them. Check out Harvard's Implicit Association Test site for an eye-opener.

Chapter Seven

Skills for Dealing with
Proactive Aggression
Users and Abusers

In this chapter you will:

- review a case study of proactive aggression in a hostel setting
- explore how an understanding of the psychology of fear can inform our practice when faced with proactive aggression
- identify skills for dealing with behaviour at the psychopathic crisis
- consider the principles of working with service users who have a history of proactive aggression
- learn about the gunpowder model for assessing the risks posed by service users with a history of proactive aggression

Imagine the following scenario:

You are a residential worker covering the night shift in a hostel for homeless men. Your colleague called in sick at the last minute so it has not been possible to arrange for cover. It is one o'clock in the morning when you hear a noise in the lounge and decide to investigate. On entering the lounge you find the room filled with smoke and a strong smell of cannabis. There are three residents huddled around a coffee table on which you notice lines of white powder, some needles and a gun. On seeing you enter, two of the residents stand up and approach you in a menacing fashion. The third, known as Doug, 45, a fairly new resident, tells them to sit down – which they do. He smiles at you and asks if there is anything he can do to help. You shake your head and withdraw to the office. On arriving there you pick up the phone to call the police. However, as you do so, the office door opens and Doug and his two associates, who are carrying knives, enter. Quietly Doug tells you to put the phone down . . .

Now we have entered an entirely different world from those of Donna (Chapter 4) or Manny (Chapter 6) – the world of proactive aggression. Unlike the examples of reactive and disturbed aggression considered so far, proactive aggression usually is:

- *Controlled* – both reactive and disturbed aggression involve a certain loss of control and the skills to deal with those forms of behaviour are largely concerned with restoring or asserting control. With proactive aggression the behaviour is usually not only in control, but controlling.
- *Purposeful* – generally perpetrators of reactive and disturbed aggression do not choose to be aggressive or violent. Rather, the aggression stems from their own inner chaos or the chaos that surrounds them. Proactive perpetrators, however, choose aggression and violence as a method and means to an end.
- *Planned* – in contrast to reactive and disturbed aggression, proactive aggression is often very carefully planned.
- *Normative* – when people engage in reactive or disturbed aggression it is usually a deviation from their normal behaviour. People who engage in proactive aggression often see violence as the norm and an integral part of their world.

These factors create considerable problems for us in dealing effectively with proactive aggression. Undoubtedly the best way to deal with this type of behaviour is to be even more proactive ourselves. Indeed the scenario involving Doug, his 'friends' and the staff member might never have happened if:

- the staff member had not been left on their own;
- the risks posed by Doug and others had been identified earlier;
- strategies for managing that risk had been implemented;
- staff had received training in managing this kind of behaviour;
- alarm systems had been put in place to alert the police of incidents within the hostel.

Nonetheless, we operate in an imperfect world and sometimes it is only after incidents such as this that we realize that to deal with proactive aggression we, and our organizations, need to be much better prepared. Even with best systems in place, however, some risk will always remain. Consequently in this chapter we will consider the following:

- the psychology of fear – understanding the mechanisms behind proactive aggression;

- skills in facing dangerous proactive aggression – what to do when faced with behaviour at the psychopathic crisis (as in the confrontation with Doug);
- establishing appropriate professional relationships – adopting a safe working style;
- skills in assessing and managing client risk – clarifying the risks posed by a service user and anticipating potential problems.

The Psychology of Fear

In Chapter 2 I mentioned that fear is our friend. It tells us

- when we are in danger;
- to wake up, pay attention, be alert;
- to activate the emergency resources in our body.

Without fear we would be blundering into all kinds of dangerous situations without any awareness of the possible risks. It is a very helpful and highly functional emotion – so long as the fear accurately reflects the danger. Obviously if we have an irrational phobia about something, or suffer from free-floating anxiety, panic disorder or post-traumatic stress disorder – then the fear is incapacitating rather than enabling.

It is the potentially incapacitating aspect of fear that proactive aggression depends upon and if we can understand how this works it might also help us to understand what we have to do in response to that aggression.

The object of proactive aggression is not to break our legs, but to induce such fear in us that we will give the aggressor what they want, for example:

- money or some other tangible reward;
- sexual gratification;
- power and dominance;
- acceptance by peers;
- control over another's actions.

The incident with Doug and the night worker in the office actually didn't involve any violence, only the fear of violence. Fear, however, is a much more powerful force than violence, and perpetrators of proactive aggression know that very well. Imagine that a service user punches you in the ribs. It is not the physical pain that is so distressing – people endure worse playing sports, falling off their bike, or in childbirth. The physical pain soon goes away, but the lingering costs might be:

- the constant ruminations;
- the flashbacks and nightmares;
- the feelings of violation;
- the loss of safety;
- the assault on one's sense of self-worth.

Violence is much more effective when it is in the mind. Doug knew that if he physically assaulted the night worker, the night worker's fear would go as their emotions were deactivated and their body's emergency system took over (see Chapter 2). Things would get very messy and Doug wouldn't achieve his goal. This is not to say that Doug and his friends would not attack the night worker, only that the attack would not result in them achieving their goal – to silence the worker and avoid getting into trouble with the police. Although Doug would like the night worker to believe that he holds all the trump cards, his hand is not that strong. Actually it is the night worker who holds the trump cards because they will always have the option of informing the police. Perpetrators of proactive aggression, however, actively set out to have us believe that all the fears are on our side, while they have none.

The next point is that fear is even more powerful if it is left to the imagination. Consider the following scenarios:

Example A A student is misbehaving in class and the teacher responds, 'Stop that at once or I'll send you to the head teacher.'
Example B A student is misbehaving in class and the teacher responds 'Stop that at once', says no more but looks directly at the student.

Although these are not necessarily examples of aggression, they do involve the use of fear to control the student's behaviour. In the first example the teacher hopes that the fear of being sent to the head teacher will result in an improvement in the student's behaviour. Of course that might well happen, but it also restricts the teacher's options and almost invites defiance – 'Go on then, send me!' In the second example, however, the teacher leaves it to the student's imagination, keeps their own options open, and offers little for the student to argue with. In the same way, 'skilled' perpetrators of proactive aggression don't really want to show their hand as it would reduce their manoeuvrability and lessen the fear.

Perhaps the following example might illustrate the power of the unknown to generate fear:

> Throughout watching the film *Silence of the Lambs* I was on the edge of my seat, holding my wife's hand and, for much of the time, not daring to look at the screen. I was terrified and yet not only was it a fictional film on a screen some 20 metres away, but actually not an awful lot happened. I later went to watch the follow-up *Hannibal*, which was far more bloody and violent – yet I didn't feel the slightest twinge of fear. Worrying about what might happen was far more powerful than the violence itself.

So the aim of proactive aggression is to deliberately induce so much fear in us that we would do almost anything to escape it – and in particular, give the aggressor what they want. Furthermore, that fear will be so much greater if they allow our minds to go rampant. It is important to understand, therefore, that in most cases our fears represent the worst case scenarios and not the probable outcomes. There will always be exceptions, but worrying about it won't change it. Proactive violence is slow in comparison to reactive and disturbed violence – intentionally so. The perpetrator wants to give us time to think, to worry and allow the fear to set in and then use this as the lever to attain their goal.

So the key points here are:

- Proactive aggression is not about the violence but the goal.
- Proactive aggression involves the deliberate induction of fear to attain that goal.
- Fear is more terrifying when left to the imagination.
- Although the aggressor will want us to think that they hold all the cards, this is rarely the case.

In the next section we will build upon these insights to look at the implications for developing a skilled response to proactive aggression.

Skills in Facing Proactive Aggression

At the point when Doug and company entered the office, we had arrived at the pivotal point, in this case the psychopathic crisis where it seems that if threats were not sufficient to attain their goal then actual violence may follow. In calling this the psychopathic crisis I am not suggesting that Doug or the other two residents are 'psychopaths'. Whatever label we might put on their heads is entirely irrelevant right now and we can leave that to others with time on their hands. Our interest is only on the immediate behaviour. Tomorrow Doug might realize what a big mistake he has made and be truly remorseful, but that doesn't help us right now.

So what can we do? The first point to make is, once again, we have to do something:

- Doing nothing allows the aggressors to take total control when they do not have our best interests at heart.
- Doing nothing will result in our fear growing to disabling levels.
- Doing nothing takes no advantage of the fact that the aggressors also may have fears, concerns and doubts despite their outward appearance.
- Doing nothing will make it more difficult to adjust emotionally and psychologically afterwards.
- The situation is already dangerous whether we do something or not.

Obviously, whatever we do carries a risk, but probably no more risk than doing nothing. Proactive aggression can make us feel very helpless so here are some alternatives:

1. *Act immediately and call for assistance*   If you have a panic button linked to a police station press it as they enter the office and before they threaten you. The aggressor's threats of violence only have power before you act.
2. *Buy time*   If you were on the phone to the police when they entered and they tell you to put it down, do so slowly and preferably not back on the hook. The longer the line stays open the more likely help will come so delay as much as you can. If the aggressors become more threatening broadcast your intentions 'Okay I'm putting it down...' This may buy a little more time.
3. *Get in first*   Try to lead the conversation rather wait for the aggressors to take over. Typically, you might say something along the lines of 'Before you say anything there is something I need to say...'
4. *Focus on the person with the greatest influence*   In this case it is Doug – you are looking to hold a dyadic conversation, not a discussion with a crowd.
5. *Sideline peripheral members of the group*   If Doug's 'friends' interject, ignore them but focus on Doug. He has already, in the lounge, demonstrated that he can control their behaviour. You might, for example say 'I thought I was talking to you Doug, not your friends here.' If Doug enjoys feeling in control this

will reinforce his position and encourage him to respond by telling his friends to let him deal with this.

6 *Explore their goal*   In this case they wanted to guarantee our silence. The more we can get them to explore this by asking questions, listening, prompting, paraphrasing, summarizing, etc., the more we will allow doubts to rise in their minds.

7 *Live to fight another day*   The only goal for us is to get out of this situation unhurt. If that means we lie through our teeth, it is a small price to pay.

8 *Offer them a damage limitation strategy*   'Listen before you say anything, nothing really bad has happened so far. You can walk away now and the police probably won't even be interested. On the other hand if you attack me ...'

9 *Talk as loudly as you reasonably can*   This will not only help you to stay in control of your own physical reactions, but you may be overheard by others who could potentially help you out. This is important to remember as some residents can feel highly protective towards staff.

10 *Keep listening and talking*   The longer it goes on in this fashion, the more doubts will enter their minds, the more opportunities there will be for help to arrive, and possibly the more confident you will begin to feel.

11 *Invite them to forecast the future*   Do not, however, under any circumstances, make threats. Threats are weak, reduce your manoeuvrability and are likely to provoke an adverse reaction. Instead you can ask 'How do think this meeting is going to end?' 'What do you imagine will happen between now and when the next shift arrives?' 'What are your plans for the next few days?' This will reduce the fear of the unknown, move the focus away from the immediate situation, and allow them to see the precariousness of their situation for themselves.

12 *Be ready to use rapid reaction skills*   These are identified in Chapter 5. With the rare exception of purely sadistic violence, the violence that follows the psychopathic crisis generally is reactive, i.e. it is driven by a sudden rise in anger, rather than the goal.

13 *Terminate contact*   Bring the situation to a conclusion as soon as possible. For example you might say 'Thank you for clarifying the situation. There is nothing left to be said, so I think it is best that we leave it at that.'

Of course, in practice the situation may not play out quite so smoothly, but that doesn't mean we shouldn't try. The important thing, however, is to keep it simple.

Establishing Appropriate Professional Relationships

In the actual incident Doug and company threatened both the staff member and their family. The staff member finished their shift and left without saying anything. The next morning they noticed a couple of residents standing outside their house. They got their family out of the area and then reported the incident. As a consequence of this incident the staff member no longer felt safe working at the hostel, or indeed in the care sector, or even in the same area.

This is a story that did not start that night in the hostel but the moment Doug entered it for the first time. This is how it started:

Doug, aged 45, arrived as a self-referral at a Direct Access Hostel. At interview he admitted to a long history of violent offences and that he had spent much of his life in prison. He had been living in an approved premises, but left when he was able to. He started drinking heavily and became street homeless and it was then that he became a vendor with The Big Issue. The staff there helped him turn his life around and get back on his feet. He says he has put his past behind him and hopes to train as a 'peer mentor' supporting prisoners after release, but he wouldn't be accepted if he was sleeping rough. He says he has also enrolled on a counselling skills course and this has opened his eyes. He is popular with the other residents and spends a lot of time talking to staff who find him good company. If there are concerns about any of the residents, he will offer to talk to them. Since his arrival two weeks ago, the atmosphere in the project has been calm.

On the surface there is nothing particularly remarkable about the situation above. We have a service user who appears to be motivated, has begun to turn his life around, and who may have a positive influence on other service users.

Doug's long history of violent behaviour, however, raises concerns that will need to be addressed if we are to help him in a way that is safe, appropriate and professional. Some of the questions we will have include:

- Is Doug being entirely honest with us, or is he just giving us the information that he knows we could access anyway?
- Is he being genuine in his decision to turn his life around, or is he merely telling the staff what he thinks they want to hear?

- If he is genuine, what are the risks that, nonetheless, he might return to the violence of his past?
- How can we assess the potential level of risk that Doug might pose to us and others?

Not only do we need to know the answers to these questions, but we owe it to Doug to do so. How can we be of any help to Doug if we are constantly questioning his word? If he is genuine, he deserves more than that.

We need to adopt an approach that is:

- *Direct*
    - If we have a question we should ask it.
    - If we have a hunch we should share it.
    - If we have a concern we should express it.
    - If we object to their behaviour we should say so.
- *Non-judgmental*   Our task is to identify possible risks not to judge the service user.
- *Honest*   This is a service user group who in the main are very good at reading people, and will probably know if we don't really believe what we say or are putting on airs.
- *Boundaried*   It is essential that we remain clear about keeping our professional role and personal life separate.

We should not avoid difficult questions or 'walk on eggshells'. Service users who have been violent in the past are generally quite resilient and will have had to talk about their offending behaviour many times to police, probation and prison staff. If there had been a referral in this case we would have some notes to check Doug's story. The lack of paperwork, however, is no impediment and we can start the assessment process off quite informally:

> 'Doug, as I am sure you are aware, we (the staff) are responsible for ensuring that your stay with us is safe, and indeed that each one of the residents here has a safe stay. You said that you had recently been staying in an approved premises, can you tell us which one that was and would you have any objections if we were to contact them?'

If Doug has no problem with this, then the first indication is that he has nothing to hide and we can benefit from any assessments or guidance the probation service may have about Doug's behaviour. At the same time we are signalling to

Doug that we are taking him seriously and are adopting an assertive approach. If he refuses, we should explore his objections, but seriously question whether this is an appropriate place for him to be. If he wants to know why we want to go into his past, we can reply along the lines:

> 'Doug, you have freely admitted that you have been violent in the past and as it turns out, past violence is the most reliable predictor of future violence. So we have a safety issue. We also accept that you want to change your life around and we want to help you with that. The process of change is difficult, however, so we need to know more about you in order that we can offer you support and to be aware should you slip back into your old ways.'

Starting out in this way not only begins the assessment process, but begins stripping back 'the unknown' which perpetrators of proactive violence, as we have seen, can use against us. It also signals that the intention is to build a strong and assertive relationship.

Multi-agency Working and Supervision

Before we go on to look in more detail at how we assess the risk posed by a service user, it is important that whenever we work with someone who may potentially be dangerous, we do not do so in isolation. Supervision that is reflective, empowering and challenging needs to be in place. This is because, with this client group, what you see is not always what you get. I, probably like many helping professionals, tend to believe what people tell me, yet we only have to look at how some of our so-called respectable politicians and bankers have behaved to be reminded of how shamelessly dishonest some people can be. Perpetrators of reactive and disturbed aggression usually wear their hearts on their sleeves while perpetrators of proactive aggression can lie low, hide, use camouflage and deceive. They can be charming and charismatic, say all the right things and make us feel good. To work with a group we need opportunities to continually reflect particularly on:

- the interpersonal dynamics operating between us and the service user;
- how we are working with them and how this is similar or different to work with other service users;
- areas that we may be avoiding or being caught up in;
- how we can make sense of the service user's behaviour, and whether alternative explanations are being prematurely dismissed.

Supervision is the obvious place for this.

The second aspect of not working in isolation is the involvement of other agencies. If a service user is known to be a risk to the public they may already be managed under the multi-agency public protection arrangements (**MAPPA**). It is essential that we know if this is the case. Even if their probation supervision/licence has expired they may still be managed by a MAPPA board and if this is the case, it is important to share information. Furthermore, if the service user is managed under MAPPA they will have conducted a thorough risk assessment on him and will be able to advise of the risks and what part you may be able to play in managing those risks. If you are unfamiliar with MAPPA you can find further details at www.facingdanger.com.

If the service user has a probation officer, then they are the obvious person to liase with. However, if a person doesn't have a criminal record, they may still be dangerous and known to the system. For this reason it is worth building good relations with local police community support officers, the anti-social behaviour teams and neighbourhood wardens. Even if the service user is unknown in the area, these teams may be able to alert you if one of your service users is getting into trouble or mixing with the wrong people.

Skills in Assessing and Managing Dangerousness

Most agencies, when they take on a new service user, will carry out an assessment that will cover risks such as violence, suicide risk, mental health, physical health, high risk areas, etc. In terms of violence it may be that it is sufficient to find out the answer to two simple questions:

- Are they known to have been violent in the past?
- Do they misuse alcohol?

If the answer is no to both questions, unless there are some obvious known factors, we don't have to go any further. If on the other hand the answer is yes, as with Doug, it may be worth looking deeper into this.

Attempts to predict who might be violent in the future have a very chequered history. Indeed there are arguments that the prediction of violence is no better than chance (Monahan 1981) and are false twice as often as they were correct. Werner et al. (1983) found that 15 psychiatrists and 15 psychologists were not even able to predict violence in an in-patient setting over a period of a week. Further research and more refined methods have led to an improvement in this situation (Hilton et al. 2006) but only in highly controlled in-patient settings and through the use of sophisticated psychometric testing. No doubt further research will lead to better methods, but at the moment we are a long way off being able to predict violence in the community settings in which many of us work. Even if we are able to get to a point where our predictions are 80 per cent accurate, what are we to do with the knowledge that we are still getting it wrong 20 per cent of the time? Should we err on the side of caution and unfairly stigmatize and unnecessarily restrict the rights of a sizeable proportion of our client group?

Most readers won't be interested in conducting a full clinical and actuarial risk assessment and will not be submitting these in court. Instead, the question we are asking is not how likely it is that the service user will be violent again, but do we have good reason to be concerned and how can those concerns be managed?

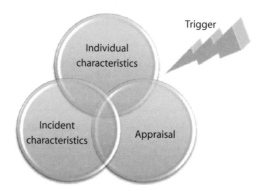

Figure 7.1. The Gunpowder Risk Assessment Model

To assist us with this I would like to introduce the 'gunpowder model' (see Figure 7.1). This is simply a way to help us think systematically about the various risk factors. The underlying principle is that violence is most likely to occur when certain factors combine in a critical way. Even the most prolifically violent people in the world actually spend the overwhelming majority of their time not being violent – but sleeping, watching TV, hanging out with their mates and so on. Something else has to come into play to explain the differences between those times when that person is violent and those when they are not. The gunpowder model proposes that violence is most likely to occur when we see three essential ingredients come together. Put any two together without the third and the combination is inert and a flame-thrower wouldn't set it off. Put in the third ingredient and the slightest spark could set it off. People who have lived a life where violence is ordinary can sometimes hold back under immense duress and yet snap at something apparently quite trivial. These three ingredients are the service user's

- profile or individual characteristics;
- characteristics of past incidents;
- appraisal of past incidents.

The ingredients will be different for each individual but once we know them for that individual we can predict that when those ingredients come together the danger will increase exponentially.

Individual Characteristics

These are those characteristics that the service user has with them all the time. They do not predict in any way when that service user will behave violently, but they do indicate the likelihood that under certain circumstances they are likely to behave violently in the future. This isn't a psychometric test but, if you find it helpful, you could score, or indeed get the service user to score, each dimension between 0 and 10. Equally, with experience you may wish to add further dimensions and/or take away others.

Here are six individual characteristics that can be useful in assessing the risk of violence:

1   Blame – to what extent do they see others as being to blame for the troubles in their life?
2   Irritability and intolerance – how easily do they become irritated by others and what can they tolerate and not tolerate?
3   Lack of empathy – how able or otherwise are they to recognize and take into account the feelings of others?
4   Reactivity – when faced with a stressor to what extent are they able to think before they act, or otherwise?
5   Skills deficits – to what extent do they lack the skills to manage stresses in their life? (Social skills, assertion skills, listening skills, problem-solving skills, conflict-resolution skills, planning skills, organizational skills, budgeting skills, etc.)
6   Substance misuse – to what extent do they misuse substances linked to violence? This refers primarily to alcohol, but also amphetamines, LSD and PCP (Roth 1994). Some prescription drugs such as fluoexetine have also been linked with increased risk of violence.

Clearly the more of these factors that come strongly into play, the more likely it is that the service user will at some point become violent again in the future.

Incident Characteristics

Here we are looking for common features that have been present in past incidents and the only way to find this out is to conduct a thorough review of those incidents with the service user and where possible with others who are familiar with incidents in the past. From this enquiry the important questions to address include:

1 What usually drives their aggression? Is it an unpleasant emotion (anger, upset, frustration, etc.), a disturbed state (including heavy use of alcohol or illegal drugs) or is it that they are violent in order to achieve a goal?
2 Who is usually the victim – an intimate partner, rival gang members, people who are perceived to be weak, anyone who shows them disrespect? Are there any people who they have never, or would never attack – women, children, their mothers, professionals, people with physical disabilities? Are there others generally involved or about when it happens?
3 When have the attacks normally occurred? How many times, how often, at what time of the day? Are there periods of their lives when they haven't been involved in any violence, for how long – and what was different about those periods?
4 Where does the violence typically take place – in the home, in pubs, at sports events, school, prison, in public areas? Is it restricted to specific geographical areas or can it occur anywhere?
5 How is it perpetrated? Is it primarily verbal, are weapons involved, how much damage generally results, how does it usually come to an end? How do they feel before, during and after the attack?

Appraisal

If you are a cognitive behavioural therapist you may wish to explore the service user's belief system in some detail (see Beck 1999; Davies 2000) but from a risk assessment perspective you might want to explore their views on the following subjects:

1 What role do they see violence as playing in society and in the world in general? Under what circumstances do they see violence as justifiable? Is there any form of violence that they consider more or less acceptable than others?
2 Do they see themselves as a violent person? How do they think other people see them? Are they happy with the way they are or do they want to change? How?
3 How do they think they have benefited from violence in the past? What has it cost them?

Trigger

The more risk factors in each category, the greater the likelihood that violence will occur in the future. However, gunpowder is not dangerous by itself, it needs a spark to become so. Consequently the final part of the assessment is to review what the triggers have been in the past. In reviewing these it is helpful also to

Table 7.1. Triggering Situations Form

Situations that have ellicted angry reactions in the past	What happened, and how likely is this to ellicit an angry reaction in the future? (0–10)	How could you handle this better, and what might help you do so?
Being confronted on rules, behaviour, breaches of contract	'I get embarrassed if this is done in front of others' 7/10	'I could ask if this could be done in private'
Being given uncomfortable feedback	'As above, plus I don't handle it well if it comes out of the blue' 7/10	'I perhaps need to take a deep breath first, but it might help if the feedback started with 'Sit down I have something to say to you'
Talking about the past	'It's not going to happen and if anyone tries to make me I am going to react' 10/10	'People shouldn't push me, but maybe I just need to tell them that calmly'
Talking about sensitive emotional issues	'I can't stand talking about that stuff – it embarrasses me' 8/10	'Maybe I have to learn to do this – just make sure no one takes the piss'
Being asked to carry a task (e.g. a personal diary)	'No problem as long as it's not something stupid' 3/10	'No problem'
Being given bad news	'My life is bad news, I can handle it' 5/10	'Just don't spring it on me and give me time on my own'
Being refused a request	'There will be a problem if I think it is unfair' 9/10	'I need to listen to the reasons before having a pop – but the reasons had better be good'
Other: 'People who keep me awake at night'	'I can take it a couple of times, after that I get murderous' 9/10	'I maybe need to sit down with that person and the staff and work out a solution to this'
Other: People who won't shut up when I am trying to watch the telly	'I am likely to take them to one side and give them a talking to' 9/10	'Maybe I should talk to them before my blood starts boiling over'

explore what would and would not lead them to feel violently against us. In this regard it can be helpful to review and complete a form like the one in Table 7.1 collaboratively with the service user.

The advantage of filling in a form such as this is that if any of these situations do arise, we can either compliment the service user on how well they managed it or remind them that this situation had already been anticipated and discussed. A final line of enquiry would be to find out if they are aware of any 'early warning signs' that might indicate to both them and us that the situation is deteriorating and becoming more dangerous.

Managing Dangerousness

So far you have read the beginning and end of the story involving Doug. Now here's the middle:

> The staff took Doug at his word without undertaking any of the investigations suggested so far in this chapter and he was treated almost as if he was an honorary staff member. In fact he wasn't known to The Big Issue at all and if the probation service had been contacted they would have discovered that after a spell in prison he often launched himself, full on into some new project that he believed would change his life. Few of these lasted more that a couple of weeks. Nonetheless, he had enrolled on a counselling skills course and had applied to train as a peer mentor. The new skills and insights from these two courses had instilled him with an almost religious zeal and he was now 'counselling' everyone he could come in contact with. He began thinking that the staff were useless and didn't have the skills that he had acquired. At the same time, it became clear that some people didn't want his help. Instead of stepping back, however, he forced his help on them with even greater vigour. At this point both the counselling skills course and peer mentor training course asked him to leave. The staff at the hostel were unaware of this because they were not in communication with the courses. Doug started drinking again and becoming increasingly bitter. By now staff were reluctant to approach him and would spend increasing amounts of time in the office. In the absence of any boundaries Doug's behaviour worsened up to the night when he and his 'friends' threatened the night worker.

This, of course, is a tragedy for everyone concerned. For the night worker and their family, for the staff who had to work in a climate of fear and intimidation, for all the people Doug forced his help upon, and for Doug himself. It appears he genuinely did want to turn his life around, that he was motivated and that he did want to help others. Unfortunately, he went about it as if enthusiasm and energy were all it took. He got hurt, withdrew and returned to his previous ways. Interestingly what happened to Doug is very similar to what happens to professionals when they burn out. They start out with unbridled enthusiasm, fail to protect themselves emotionally, get hurt, withdraw emotionally, lose interest, start blaming others, become cynical and then collapse (Brown and Bourne 1996).

Instead things might have turned out very differently if:

- the staff had developed a direct, honest, non-judgmental relationship with him from the outset;
- they had contacted other agencies from the start and maintained that contact throughout;
- the staff had been proactive and initiated contact with Doug rather than waiting for him to come to them;
- Doug had been fully engaged in an assessment of his past behaviour;
- agreements had been made about how he would deal with situations that could potentially trigger aggression in the future.

If those things had happened, then the staff could have

- encouraged him to work towards his goals in a slower, surer way;
- monitored the process and given him continuous feedback and support;
- known that he had been asked to leave the courses and helped him find other avenues to pursue;
- challenged him safely when his behaviour began to deteriorate.

Summary

In this chapter we have explored the very different way in which proactive aggression presents itself from both reactive and disturbed aggression. Specific skills are suggested for managing the pivotal point for proactive aggression (the psychopathic crisis) where threats and intimidation might easily spill over into violence. Difficult proactive aggression is covert and predatory and so often doesn't reveal itself until the psychopathic crisis has arrived and threatens to become dangerous. For this reason, the skills in working with proactive aggression largely centre around establishing a strong and appropriate style of working, assessing the risks with the service user and intervening proactively as soon as signs of trouble appear.

Top Tips

- People who engage in proactive aggression form a very challenging client group. It is essential to develop a respectful but assertive working style with very clear boundaries.
- It is essential to have good supervision and to be in continuous contact with all of the other agencies who are involved with the service user.
- Whereas it is not helpful to ask questions when dealing with reactive and disturbed aggression, here it is essential in order to slow the behaviour down, reduce the aggressor's manoeuvrability and sow the seeds of doubt.
- It is essential to do a good assessment of the risk that the service user might pose to you and others. It is important to carry out this assessment with the service user involved as this helps diminish 'the fear of the unknown' and gives legitimacy to any concerns you may later wish to raise with the service user.
- Respond proactively as soon as you detect any worsening in their behaviour. The longer you delay the more difficult and potentially dangerous that behaviour is likely to be.

Chapter Eight
Putting it Together
Skills in Context

> **In this chapter you will:**
> - explore procedural issues such as risk assessments, lone-working and office-based procedures
> - identify strategies for working collaboratively with colleagues to contain a crisis
> - consider skills dealing with incidents in a variety of group settings
> - review some of the major factors in supporting staff following an incident

Throughout this book I have been at pains to look at facing danger not in some abstract way but in the context in which professionals encounter that danger. The primary focus of the discussion has been on the skills while some of the issues have been skimmed over. In this chapter we will look in greater detail at some of those issues which include:

1. risk assessment;
2. lone-working;
3. office-based policies and procedures;
4. working alongside colleagues;
5. dangerous behaviour in group settings;
6. staff support and post-incident care.

Here I will try to highlight those issues that I consider make the greatest difference and to introduce a few ideas that may not be available elsewhere in the literature and that may provoke some thought.

Risk Assessment

In the previous chapter we looked at assessing the risk posed by a specific service user. Here, I would like to look at a more situational type of risk assessment. Figure 8.1

	Low Risk (0–3)	Medium Risk (4–6)	High Risk (7–10)
Client Variables			
1. History of Violence	None	Verbal	Physical
2. Impulse Control	In control	Over-controlled controlling	Under-controlled
3. Tolerance Threshold	High	Medium	Low
4. Current Major Stressors	None known	One	Several
5. Recent Losses	None	One	Several (inc. psychological)
6. Physical Illness	None	Mild	Prolonged, with pain and uncertain outcome
7. Disorientation	None/little	Confused	Deluded
8. Personal Style	Responsive, co-operative	Difficult, resistant, antagonistic	Disordered, abusive
9. Drug/Alcohol Usage	None	Reasonable	Excessive/addictive
10 Sexual History	In a stable relationship	Unsatisfactory relationships	Includes sexual offences
Worker-Client Contact			
11. Significance for Client	Important, but not vital	Unimportant	Vital, excessive/Not known
12. Worker's role	Assisting client	Assessing client	Unwanted intrusion
13. Recent of Contact	Same day	Recent past	None
14. Previous Contact	Good	Fair	Poor/none
15. Likelihood of prejudice	Little	Covert	Overt
16. Worker's stress	Optimally stressed	Under-stressed	Over-stressed
Situation			
17. Route to Visit/Ease of escape	Secure	Only momentary hazards	Prolonged vulnerability
18. Presence of Others	Others that may assist	None. or unknown	Others that may be a hostile
19. Unusual circumstances	None	Some, but understandable	Significant unexplained factors
20. Incidence of violence in locality	Low	Average	High
TOTALS			

Figure 8.1. A Situational Risk Assessment

shows one form of risk assessment which might be carried out before beginning work with a service user. Although it has a scoring system, the scores mean nothing other than the higher the score the more care should be taken to ensure the safety of staff – it is not in any way a validated psychometric instrument. It was originally designed in anticipation of a staff member making home visits, although it can easily be adapted for client contact in other settings. It is important, however, that it is not seen as a static assessment but that it is constantly reviewed in the light of experience, new information and changing circumstances.

Of course any assessment will be worthless or worse unless it is taken seriously, supported by senior management and integrated into practice. Carrying out an assessment and then filing it away is dangerous.

Lone-working

Assuming that some form of risk assessment has been undertaken, it is important to recognize that risk is dynamic and changeable. The risk does not just arise from the professional nature of the work with the service user but from all the other variables involved in being out in the community alone. Walking through estates troubled with gang culture, encountering unexpected higher risk service users on our way to an otherwise straightforward visit, visiting a service user only to discover the presence of friends and family, visiting a service user whose mental health has deteriorated significantly since our last involvement – many things can happen between assessment and the outcome.

Those are not reasons to abandon assessment, simply recognition that there are far too many variables to factor in. Personally and theoretically my view is that the best indicator of immediate risk is the sensation you get from your body – that gut reaction, or seventh sense. As we saw earlier, this is most likely to be the activation of the limbic system via Le Doux's 'low road' – our personal and ever-present radar. Of course if you always feel anxious that that might simply indicate that you are an anxious person. If you feel nauseous approaching a visit but had too much to drink last night and then ate a dodgy kebab, that could also be an explanation. Otherwise it is an indication that your thalamus has spotted danger, activated the limbic system leaving the frontal cortex puzzled and playing catch up. So what do we do?

We live in a technological era and when many of the texts on personal safety were written most people didn't even have mobile phones. Technology – smartphones, GPS tracking devices, webcams, etc. – however, is only as good as the people who operate it. We will revisit the office or organizational back-up for staff lone-working in the next section. Here I will focus only on what the lone-working staff member can do.

Going back to the walk-through case study in Chapter 4, Pat's instincts on arriving at the property were that something was very wrong although there appeared to be little evidence to support this – the young woman was welcoming, the house was clean, there was no sign of drug or alcohol misuse, no one else untoward seemed present. Pat's cognitive processing – 'don't be silly', 'pull yourself together' and so forth – effectively deactivated her radar and alarm system.

Instead, I would advocate that this should be seen as the best and most effective risk screening tool – providing we are in reasonably good mental health. If this sounds a little woolly and you haven't had a chance to read Chapters 1 and 2, you might be interested that a study by Raio et al. (2012) – widely reported in the press and online – showed that we can sense danger even when we are consciously unaware of it – just like Spiderman! Once this 'sense' has been experienced, of course we shouldn't immediately run for the hills. Instead we should investigate and re-assess the situation.

Here are some simple precautions that can be taken:

- Make sure that you have the mobile telephone number of the person who you are about to visit. These days most people have a mobile phone. Some rural areas still have little connectivity but this will change in the near future.
- If possible call the person you are about to visit about five minutes before you arrive – whether or not you suspect danger – it's just good manners and avoids them feeling surprised or embarrassed by your arrival.
- Use this opportunity to assess if it's inconvenient, or if they are drunk or high – you should be able to get a good sense of that on the phone.
- You may also be able to assess their compliance – you could ask them to bring their partner/flatmate/associate to the phone, or maybe ask if they could turn the music down so that you can talk. Their response should give a good idea of the risks ahead.
- If you can't make telephone contact, it may be worthwhile contacting other professionals before proceeding – the community nurse, GP, housing officer, social worker, neighbourhood warden, support worker, care worker, etc. They may be aware of any important changes in circumstances.
- If that doesn't clarify the potential risk then call your manager or experienced colleague to talk the situation through.
- Further options include talking to neighbours, local residents and staff working in the local area to see if they are aware of any recent concerns.

- If there is a statutory requirement to make the visit then police assistance should be requested – otherwise it may be better to put a calling card and note through the letterbox suggesting that the service user makes contact with you.
- Should you decide to go ahead with the visit alert colleagues giving your location and arrange for them to call you back in five minutes.
- There are also numerous commercial systems which can track your whereabouts, record conversations and alert key individuals or the police if there is a concern.
- If you have arrived by road, where possible, park the vehicle in a way that would allow you to get away easily if need be.
- After knocking on the door, take a few steps away from the door. This would make it easier to withdraw should there be some hostility or if the service user has an aggressive dog. It also signals to the householder that you have no intention of forcing your way in.
- If there is any doubt at the door simply make an excuse and withdraw. For example, 'Sorry, I left my diary in the car'.

Do not enter the property until you have:

- seen the person you have come to see;
- clarified the purpose of the visit;
- ascertained their state of mind and attitude to your visit;
- ensured that there is no one else present that might cause a concern.

On entering the property:

- keep an eye out for anything unusual;
- take note of any routes out of the property;
- do not sit down until you are sure that everything is okay.

If the situation changes, for example if someone unexpected enters the room, it is better to stand up and offer to return when it is more convenient. For example, you might say, 'Listen, I hadn't realized that you had company. Actually I'm running a bit late, perhaps we can do this another time?'

Of course you can do all of this and still end up in danger, but ensuring your safety is part of your professional role, your responsibility to family, friends and other people who rely upon you and your organization's legal responsibility.

In-house Procedures (for your office or centre)

In the incident involving Manny it was quite clear that the office was unprepared to deal with any untoward incidents that might occur in the reception area. Many offices have panic alarms but these are only as good as the procedures that go with them and the awareness staff have of those procedures. By law we have to have fire alarm drills and yet it is far more likely that an untoward incident will occur at reception – so why do so few offices have panic alarm drills?

Obviously each office or centre is different so it is not possible to prescribe a set of procedures for each one, but there are basic principles that should be in place:

1 Everyone in the office should know what the alarm sounds like, where it will be heard and by whom.
2 Staff, even a temp who is just covering for the day, should be told that they should activate the alarm if they feel they need help and that they should err on the side of safety. They should also know that they will not be criticized or get into trouble for doing so.
3 One member of staff needs to be responsible for coordinating the collective efforts. This will primarily involve allocating tasks to staff members, i.e. who should
    a   call for assistance, whether it be an ambulance, the police or security;
    b   remove guests from the waiting area;
    c   prevent members of the public from entering;
    d   provide back-up for the receptionist;
    e   distract or divert an aggressor should a colleague be in trouble;
    f   calm or reassure others.
4 There should be a clear procedure for staff to follow once the alarm has been activated – and one that results in the minimum number of people being involved. What is not helpful is for everyone to rush to wherever the alarm has been sounded.
5 The only priority is personal safety – if that means the service users wrecks the waiting area it is a small price to pay – insurance will cover that.

Further information and resources on workplace policies and procedures can be found at www.facingdanger.com.

Staff should also know how to work together in a crisis without shouting over, or contradicting one another. This is addressed next.

Working Alongside Colleagues

Different staff have different styles and when working together to contain a crisis there is always the danger that they may get in the way of one another. Unfortunately we can't always predict when trouble will occur and when it does we often have no time to discuss with our colleagues how it might best be handled. In the incident with Manny staff talked over and contradicted one another leading not only to a net increase in the chaos and confusion but also to some ill-feeling and resentment afterwards.

Good teamwork is essential especially if you work in pairs, or if you work in a residential service, a prison, hospital ward or any other setting where other colleagues are usually present. Ideally the principles of crisis teamwork should be clarified at the outset as part of each staff member's induction. Alternatively, if you are involved in a statutory multi-agency situation, such as the removal of a child or the mental health assessment of an individual, the professional approach is to discuss with agency partners how the situation will be dealt with should everything 'kick off'. Obviously these guidelines might vary from place to place and service to service but the following might give a flavour of what could be appropriate:

1 When an incident takes places usually the person who will deal with it in the first instance will be whoever is closest at hand. Obviously this may not be the most senior, experienced or even most competent (in handling dangerous behaviour) member of staff. Nonetheless, unless they give a clear signal that they need assistance, or feel out of their depth, other staff members should not intervene even if they feel that they have a better idea about how to handle the situation. It can also feel tempting to do or say something in order to show support. However, something is already being done so either your intervention unnecessarily repeats that, or is in some way different, and that is the problem – it adds confusion and undermines the first member of staff. The only circumstances in which other staff should intervene are:

   a if the first staff member indicates they need that help;
   b if they are in immediate danger;
   c if they are behaving in a grossly unprofessional way;
   d *but never because you think you have a different or better approach.*

2 If the aggressor tries to draw you in, do not answer any questions or attempt to take over. Instead it is better to refer them back to your colleague who was originally dealing with them by saying something such as 'Talk to Pat' or 'Pat asked you a question' or 'Pat is dealing with you'. In this way you show

confidence in your colleague and offer them tacit support. It also keeps the situation simple, which is our goal.

3 If your colleague gives a direction that you do not fully agree with – maybe they shout 'Get out' rather too forcibly – and the service user asks you what you think about that, decline to offer a view. To repeat what your colleague has already said might come across as bullying, while to express it differently simply adds an extra source of confusion into the mix. Instead it is enough to say 'You have heard what has been said'. Afterwards you can review how the situation was handled, and if it is appropriate an apology can be offered to the service user.

4 While your colleague is dealing with the incident, the task of other staff members will be to manage the environment. This will include clearing the area of bystanders, removing objects that could be used as weapons, preventing others from entering the area and calling for police assistance if necessary.

5 If there is more than one staff member looking on, one should concentrate on the staff member who is dealing with the incident in order to ensure that they are okay and to take their cue from them. The other should be watching the service user in case there is a risk of which your colleague is unaware. Other staff should withdraw, but remain available, to avoid creating an 'audience effect'.

There is nothing complicated about these 'rules' but if your colleague knows what to expect from you, they can devote their energies to dealing with the situation rather than worrying about unsolicited interventions from colleagues. It also reduces the risk of recriminations between staff of the kind 'Why didn't you back me up?' or 'I felt undermined by you', which could have a corrosive effect on team morale.

Dangerous Behaviour in Group Settings

Often when incidents occur there will be onlookers, bystanders and sometimes more than one aggressor. Obviously in these situations we will be outnumbered and our resources severely stretched and so on the face of it this is not a very promising situation. Of course if large numbers mobilize themselves against us there may be very little we can do as we saw during the riots at Strangeways Prison, Manchester and throughout the prison service in the early 1990s. That, however, is not a reason to be defeatist and indeed the more dire our situation the less we have to lose in trying something.

Figure 8.2. A Typology of Group Violence

Essentially there are four main group scenarios involving violence. Violence in a group can be by the group or in and towards the group. Whichever way, that group might be organized or disorganized. These dichotomies provide us with a taxonomy of group violence as illustrated in Figure 8.2.

In each case the main priority will be to reduce the number of people involved wherever possible. If this can be achieved to the point there is only one person to deal with then we can return to the skill sets outlined in the preceding chapters.

Principles in Dealing with Group Violence

The primary focus, with the exception of the gang scenario, will be on the group and the use of clear authoritative instructions to clear the area. Our professional role confers a certain degree of authority in its own right and in a crisis people are often desperate for leadership and direction and will often follow anyone who seems to know what to do. Ever since the dramatic and iconic experiments of Milgram and Zimbardo the social psychology literature has been replete with studies looking at obedience to authority. Giving unequivocal commands to leave the area lessens the need for onlookers to feel that they should be doing something and offers a face-saving way of withdrawing. If there is time, it may be better to confer helpful roles on bystanders, rather than instruct them. For example you could ask the more able-bodied people to assist those who may have mobility issues, or ask them to call for assistance.

When faced with an organized hostile group, such as a gang, the same strategy does not apply. It is not that we wouldn't dearly love the gang to disappear, it's just that they already have a leader and they are unlikely to take commands from us. Here instead our focus should not be on the gang, but the gang leader who shouldn't be difficult to pick out as it's likely to be the person immediately facing us! Since the 'gang leader' is the one with the influence, our efforts need to be focussed on them in a dyadic relationship while sidelining gang members. If during our dialogue other gang members try to join in, probably the best thing to do is to ignore them but tell the gang leader 'I thought I was talking to you, not your friend here.' This validates the gang leader's role while sidelining unhelpful interference from the group. It also takes the gang leader down the line of least resistance as it will be easier, and offers more kudos, to assert their ability to deal with us directly than have their authority undermined by junior gang members. Having established the dyadic interaction, albeit surrounded by the gang, we can return to the skills outlined for dealing with reactive aggression. If the levels of arousal are low we use defusing skills; if it is becoming heated then we use the de-escalating skills and if it all kicks off it's the rapid reaction skills. On the other hand, if on listening to them they have some demand (proactive aggression) we follow the procedures for dealing with the psychopathic crisis outlined in Chapter 7.

In the case of chaotic group violence such as a riot the obvious point to note is that we would have to have done something quite extraordinary to become the focus of that riot. The risk is being caught up in the chaos and so the only sensible advice is to get out of the way and take any vulnerable people with you.

Dealing with Multiple Service Users

The group examples that are more likely to be relevant to us as helping professionals are those when an incident takes place in the presence of other service users as would be the case if you were a teacher in school, a group facilitator or a staff member working on a ward, hostel or prison. The difference here is that you would have a pre-existing relationship with the group members individually and as a whole and that you are in a position of authority. In that sense much of the work should have been done well before the 'group incident' takes place. Essentially if each service user can sense that you are competent, can demonstrate absolutely clear personal, professional and organizational boundaries and have a genuine interest in them as a person then you will be in a good position to deal with anything that arises within the group. I have already referred several times throughout this book to managing boundaries effectively and you really shouldn't be in this work if you can't show a genuine interest in the people you serve.

Being competent in handling chaotic and dangerous group behaviour, however, is rather more elusive. Here I refer not to competence in general – your ability to write a court report will not help you as mayhem breaks out – but leadership competence in group settings. Throughout my career I have always been fascinated by the way in which some professionals are able to assume leadership and take control of groups almost effortlessly, while some struggle valiantly and yet fail. The most obvious example would be the contrasting fortunes of different teachers dealing with the same groups of students – you might want to reflect on your own time at school. One teacher walks into the class and everyone has their books out and is ready to work hard. Another teacher walks into the same classroom and chaos reigns. This cannot be about the students as they were the same in each case – the variable is the teacher. Of course many factors will come into play and I do not wish to oversimplify or minimize the efforts and psychological torment faced by the struggling teacher. It does, however, seem to me that the difference between the two teachers is significant and yet not as huge as one might suspect.

Confidence is naturally a large part of it, but where does confidence come from? It resides within us but its source comes from the world outside. If I deliver a training course and get really good feedback then the next time I deliver that course I will feel more confident and might get even better feedback. If on the other hand, I receive highly critical feedback then I might lose confidence and the next time I deliver the course I may come across as anxious, unsure of my material and indecisive and the feedback may be even more critical. So confidence is critical but unfortunately it is not available on prescription.

Some years back, a number of colleagues and I came up with the idea that the ability to manage group behaviour in a crisis was not determined by either a person's style nor was it related to their overt behaviour. Late night discussions led us to identify three covert micro-skills. These 'skills', which I have taken every possible opportunity to try out and observe in practice, do not depend on personality or type. Furthermore, throughout this book I have emphasized the importance of the notion that people can only effectively resist influences on their behaviour of which they are aware. If you tell me to sit down, I can easily resist by telling you where you might go. On the other hand if I was not so aware that you were trying to direct my behaviour I might be less able to resist. These 'under-the-radar skills' in relation to group behaviour are **patterning, modulating** and **limiting** (see Figure 8.3).

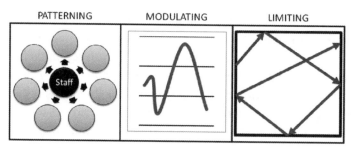

Figure 8.3. The Three Critical Micro-skills for Managing Group Situations

Patterning

Patterning refers to the way in which the staff member initially non-verbally aligns the communications between themselves and the others as they enter a group setting. The first point is that this is done non-verbally so that although others might sense that something has happened, they will find it difficult to argue with or reject. The idea is to place oneself at the 'hub' of all the communications, with those communications radiating out like the spokes on a wheel. This involves making brief but immediate and direct contact with each person in the group setting. If it is a staff member starting a shift on a ward, the first thing they do, even before attending the handover meeting, is to make direct eye contact with each patient and maybe say no more than 'Hi', although using their name helps (e.g. 'Hello Ade'). This simple and absolutely natural device immediately signals an interest in them, opens a line of communication, shows confidence and ensures that the patient knows that they are visible. If the staff member walks into a group setting, it may be enough to make direct eye contact with each group member at the outset. I'm not sure it matters too much if the eye contact is intense, soft or whatever, but it should be direct and held long enough for the other person to know that contact has been made, but not so long as to make them feel uncomfortable. My own sense is that staff who walk straight past service users, or enter group settings without first making direct contact with those present, end up finding it very difficult to regain the ground they lost at the beginning. Indeed it seems to me that staff who regularly 'pattern' often have a presence that is immediately noticed on entering a group setting. In relation to dealing with danger in group settings this is critical – we must become the hub of all the communications otherwise we are just a number in a crowd.

Obviously, I am not suggesting that we should always demand that we are the centre of attention. The aim of most good group work is for the facilitator's presence to go almost unnoticed. It is, however, important to return to become the 'hub' when needed – and you can't return to a place you've never been!

Modulating

Modulating is the way in which we, again non-verbally, orchestrate the levels of arousal and activity within the group. This is only possible if you have already patterned the communications within that setting so that group members can take their cue from you. People don't generally like being corrected or told that their behaviour is unacceptable but do seek approval and are continually assessing the reactions of others to their behaviour. For the most part this is managed unconsciously and without thought. Nonetheless, it is extremely important that other people in the group 'know where you stand' and the more secure they are in this knowledge the less they are likely to act out or test you out. The skill in modulating is therefore to be able to send out a continuous stream of low level non-verbal cues to signal that to people in the group. In other words it is important to be non-verbally expressive – smiles, shrugs, raised eyebrows, winks, hand gestures, eye contact and so forth. As behaviour becomes increasingly unacceptable these modulating signals will increase in intensity allowing group members to modify that behaviour without appearing to back down. An everyday example of a 'modulating signal' would be the 'look' that many children will recognize on their mother's face, which I think many will agree is far more powerful than words.

The importance of these modulating signals can be seen when the staff member doesn't give out these signals. It might be that they are anxious, don't want the service user to know this and so try to hide their emotions by keeping a straight face. The problem with this is that the service user may misread the 'stony face' as hostile or disinterested, or may act out to elicit a less confusing signal. Furthermore, when the staff member does have to enforce some limits on the service user's behaviour it may come as a bolt from the blue and consequently evoke an angry or upset response.

Limiting

When faced with an unruly group it is understandable that sometimes staff will feel undermined and under resourced. Clearly there is a need to place limits on people's behaviour in a group setting; however, the use of sanctions and threats is possibly the worst way to go about this. We are talking here of the immediate management of the behaviour, the short story, not the longer-term decisions that may follow further down the line. If one student assaults another then if the rules say they must be excluded, then they must be excluded. However, if a student looks like they are about to hit another student in class it is not helpful to use threats to manage their behaviour. People rarely back down in the face of threats and instead it often increases their resolve: 'Put that chair down now, or I'll report you to the Head.' 'Go on then, report me!' This is much more likely in a group setting where a climb down might be publicly humiliating, or they may enjoy playing to the crowd.

There is another problem in using threats to control behaviour in a group setting and that is that it signals to the group that you cannot manage the behaviour on your own, but need a big stick to do so – and those big sticks will never be big enough. Even if it does work on this one occasion it sets up an unhelpful dynamic for the future. If behaviour is controlled by sanctions, what about those lower levels of behaviour which although inappropriate do not merit sanctions? It's a path to a situation where fire-fighting and crisis management become the norm. Instead it is better that we are able to convey that the source of our influence is internal rather than external and this is achieved by following the dictum that has run throughout this book 'you always do something, not more, less but always something'. Just as with our discussion of personal boundaries the rule here is that if we want someone to do something, we should just ask or tell them to do it and no more. This is particularly important in a group context.

The point of all this is that if we can recognize the importance of these micro-skills in our day-to-day practice with our client group we may be far better placed to be able to manage any crisis that emerges within that group.

Staff Care and Post-incident Support

As we draw to the end of this book we come to the part that may be the most important. However skilful any of us might be, we cannot rule out becoming the victim of some form of violation. We work in the 'people professions' and perhaps our only true instrument is ourselves – so we should ensure that we keep ourselves in good condition through good supervision, training, support and a healthy lifestyle.

If we are tired and stressed, overwhelmed by demands and feel unsupported then we will not be able to perform as a skilled professional and all the words in this book will not help us. We will make mistakes and when things go wrong we will not have the resources to deal with the crisis. Furthermore, if we wait until either we or a colleague is involved in a serious incident our attempts to help and support are likely to be clumsy and fumbling. If, on the other hand, the ground-work has been laid, when trauma enters our worlds we may be much better able to deal with it.

For me, these are the important issues:

- All staff should receive regular supervision that is supportive, reflective, empowering and developmental. The aim of supervision is to enable the staff member to function at their optimal level of competence within the parameters set out by their job role, profession and organization. It is not a place for paperwork.
- Supervision should create a climate in which the staff member's stress levels can be monitored and managed without judgment. Brown and Bourne (1996) propose that regular 'stress checks' are incorporated into supervision and that the risk of 'professional burnout' is actively managed through close examination of the way in which the staff member opens themselves up to and protects themselves from the interpersonal aspects of the work.
- Each of us is different and will respond differently to support when it is offered. Supervision offers an opportunity for the staff member to explore what forms of support they have found helpful and unhelpful in the past and what they would want in the future. In that way each staff member can work towards developing a personal 'crisis plan' which can be shared with colleagues. In the immediate aftermath of an incident some people want to surround themselves with people they feel close to, have lots of hugs and permission to scream, shout and cry, while others prefer to be left on their own.
- Although the first criterion for the diagnosis of PTSD is the stressor criterion which states that 'the person had to have experienced, witnessed, or was confronted with an event that involved actual or threatened death or serious injury, or a threat to the physical of the person or others' – the absence of such a major stressor should not imply that the subjective experience is any less traumatic. Being spat at can be more traumatic than being threatened with a knife. The thing about violence and trauma is that both are overwhelmingly psychological. The worst things about violence are the worry and anxiety that precede it and the inability to escape from the memories afterwards. In comparison, the cuts, bruises and physical pain subside into insignificance. It is important that managers and colleagues do not confuse the magnitude of the incident with the amount of distress generated.
- After any incident it is natural to ruminate over the events, ask lots of 'why' questions and to blame or be critical of ourselves and our actions. In this very sensitive period it is important that others don't compound that sense of blame through thoughtless comments like 'What did you do to provoke him?'; 'We all make mistakes…'; 'Did you follow company policy?'

An investigation or a review may be necessary but now is not the time and people come first.

- Trauma can be thought of as a rupture with the past. We don't continually re-invent the world but instead we learn to make assumptions about ourself, others and the world we live in – it's what makes us who we are and keeps things predictable. A trauma shatters those assumptions and creates a break from everything we thought we knew. A bereavement can be thought of as a loss of someone close to you; a trauma is a loss of oneself – and both are processes of loss and adjustment. That process can be rocky, so just because one day your colleague seems fine doesn't mean that the journey is over.

- Often a lot of support is offered in the immediate aftermath of the incident when the staff member may not feel they can use it. Later when they realize how much they need it, it is often no longer there. Supervision isn't the place for therapy, but it does play an important role in monitoring how well the staff member is adjusting post-trauma.

- Staff should not be rushed into counselling or psychological treatment. Trauma counselling received a bad press in the late 1990s and in the early part of this century with claims that far from helping people adjust after a major incident it exacerbated their symptoms. This actually was the way some limited research was misrepresented in the press. It is true that some researchers (Bledsoe 2003) did find that when emergency staff personnel were required to attend a very specific debriefing procedure in the immediate aftermath of a major incident, some found it unhelpful. This, however, was a one off group debriefing facilitated by people who were not trained therapists or qualified mental health professionals. This is not the same as trauma counselling, which is conducted on an individual basis, only at the staff member's request, and provided by a qualified practitioner. Nonetheless, immediate support should come from those that are closest – friends, family, colleagues and supervisor. In the days following the incident the staff member needs to regain their moorings, re-establish relationships and routines and deal with the immediate repercussions of the incident. Their manager should identify possible sources of psychological help in order to cut down on any delays should the staff member request it at a later stage.

- The staff member should be encouraged to contact their union or professional association and be given access to legal advice should they need it. They should also be given information about 'normal reactions to traumatic events' to help normalize their experience. Further details can be found at www.facingdanger.com.

- Even if the staff member was grossly responsible for the incident, they still have the right to be treated with the same care, dignity and respect. Disciplinary matters are separate from support needs and shouldn't be confused.
- In most cases, it would be hoped that the staff member will recover fully and may even come out feeling stronger. However, sometimes a change of scene and role may be needed and the staff member's organization has a responsibility to facilitate this as far as is possible. If I was the staff member who knocked on Donna's door and then was attacked with a knife, I am sure that, however well my treatment went, I would no longer wish to lone-work or make home visits – but I would also feel really hard done by if that left me unemployed.

Just a final note to end on. This book is about skills. Throughout, the underlying dictum has been 'you don't do more, you do less, but you do something' and our explorations have been about identifying what that simple something is in a range of different professional contexts and in the face of different behaviours. We can do everything by the letter and still get attacked – there are no guarantees – but no one deserves to be attacked and no one is responsible for being attacked. Nor is it a part of our professional role, although it is a hazard that accompanies our professional role. Hazards need to be managed – by us, by our colleagues, our managers and our organizations.

Summary

Although the main part of this book has been concerned with identifying skills in responding to reactive, disturbed and proactive aggression, in this chapter we have looked in greater detail at some of the issues that run alongside these skills. However skilful we are it is difficult to practise in a skilled way if our organization lacks policies and procedures to support that practice, or if we are not well supervised, or if colleagues undermine us in a crisis. This chapter, therefore has been about putting those skills in context and, where possible, providing guidance.

Top Tips
- Skills are not context free and have to be supported by policies and procedures.
- Ensure that your organization has clear, well-communicated and supported policies and procedures for risk assessment, lone-working and work place safety.

- Ensure you are clear about how to work collaboratively with colleagues in a crisis and that this has been discussed and clarified beforehand.
- Consider the kinds of group setting within which you might have to deal with dangerous behaviour and be clear about the principles of effective group control.
- Ensure that you operate in a supportive team environment, with good supervision in which personalized post-incident support plans have been clarified and communicated.

Glossary

Acute stress response The body's physical responses to immediate danger. Originally described as fight or flight, but now describing a sequence of hierarchical body choices – focus, flight, fight, freeze.

Alexithymia The inability to put words to emotions.

Amygdala An organ within the limbic system associated with the processing of emotion.

Automacity The degree to which action takes place spontaneously and without thought.

Behavioural approach Refers to the idea that it is better to ignore negative behaviour and reinforce positive behaviour. However, in the short term, ignoring behaviour leads to an increase in that behaviour.

Broken record technique A skill drawn from assertiveness training which simply involves repeating the same statement.

Catastrophic reaction Similar to 'temper tantrums' but occurs when a person becomes highly confused and cannot understand what is happening to them.

Cathartic approach Sometimes 'the cathartic fallacy' refers to the discredited idea, in relation to aggression, that it is better to get it out of your system. If anything, the more anger you express, the more angry you get.

Command hallucinations Powerful auditory hallucinations that bully the hearer to follow their instructions.

Confusion A state where a person is able to process the information that they are receiving. It is closely associated with panic and catastrophic reactions.

De-escalating skills Skills used as reactive aggression approaches the dysphoric tilt, but hasn't yet become violent.

Defusing skills Low level, good customer care skills used to minimize the risk of reactive aggression taking place.

Difficult, Disturbing and Dangerous Behaviour The training course that accompanies this book (www.dangerousbehaviour.com).

Dissociation A disconnection between mind and body, like dreaming, hypnosis and when we act without thought.

Disturbed aggression Aggression driven by some form of psychological disturbance – confusion, hallucinations, delusion or paranoia.

Dysphoric crisis The pivotal point for reactive aggression. As the emotion and tension rise it becomes increasingly difficult to continue behaving in the same way as their cognitive faculties become impaired. This point is also sometimes referred to as the Vacuum because psychologically the demands increase upon the aggressor and their resources diminish, seconds can feel like an eternity and with nowhere to go. It is as if they are in a vacuum – and one that needs to be filled fast.

Emergency psychological processes Psychological processes that occur in parallel with the acute stress response and including focussed attention, rapid processing of incoming data, deactivation of emotional responses, enhanced memory, state dependent learning and distorted perception of time.

Empathy The ability to put oneself in someone else's shoes and relate to how they feel.

Focussing response The first reaction preceding the acute stress response and the emergency psychological processes.

Force-field analysis A way of looking at how driving forces are counterbalanced by restraining force to create a dynamic tension. The idea was first developed by the social psychologist Kurt Lewin.

Frontal cortex The thinking part of the brain.

Front-end rapid reaction skills Skills used immediately as a crisis occurs and before thought takes place. They are largely designed to manage one's own body reaction and avoid actions that might increase personal danger.

Hippocampus A part of the limbic system responsible for declarative memory. This is where the survival schemas in particular, the rapid reaction skills, will be stored.

Hypothalamus The part of the brain that sends hormonal signals from the brain to the body. In terms of danger, it will send those signals to the adrenal glands where adrenaline and cortisol – the stress hormones – will prepare the body for action.

Implicit Association Tests A series of tests to reveal biases that we may not think we have. Unlike psychometric tests these are not influenced by knowing the right answers and can be undertaken freely and anonymously online.

Implied Suggestions An under-the-radar skill used to suggest that someone might already be complying with a demand without actually saying so. In the context of responding to violence, it is used alongside the broken record technique and simply involves the words 'that's it', or 'good', or 'thanks'.

Instant Aggression Model The model underpinning this book which analyses an aggressive or violent act as it happens rather than how it might be understood in review.

Lima syndrome The mirror image of the Stockholm syndrome where abusers become attached to those they abuse.

Limbic system A group of brain structures including the thalamus, amygdala, hypothalamus and hippocampus that closely connect the cerebral cortex with the autonomic nervous system and that is sometimes referred to as 'the Lizard Brain'.

Limiting A non-verbal skill of placing limits on group behaviour from an internal locus of control.

Low road A term coined by LeDoux to describe a neural pathway short-circuiting the frontal cortex and activating the limbic system directly. This allows us to act without thought. This is a fast but rough and ready route.

MAPPA The multi-agency public protection arrangements used for monitoring dangerous offenders in the community.

Modulating A non-verbal skill aimed at sending signals out to group members approval or otherwise of group activity.

Mood-matching The idea that communication flows best between people who are at the same emotional level. Not to be confused with mirroring the same behaviour.

Parasympathetic nervous system The part of the central nervous system activated when getting ready to attack. It is like the body's braking system.

Passivity experiences A psychotic state, usually associated with schizophrenia, where a person believes their behaviour is being controlled by someone else.

Patterning A non-verbal skill aimed at arranging the interactions in a group setting such that you are at the hub of those interactions.

Pivotal point The point where the aggressor's behaviour is in the balance between escalating and perpetrating aggression. At this point it may take very little to tilt the behaviour either way.

Proactive aggression Purposeful or instrumental aggression where the aggression is deliberately perpetrated to achieve a goal.

Psychopathic crisis The pivotal point for proactive aggression. This is the point where threats and intimidation no longer feel sufficient to achieve their goal, and violence is chosen as the best way to that end.

Psychosis containment skills Skills used to contain disturbed aggression. These build upon and supplement rapid reaction skills.

Psychotic crisis The pivotal point for disturbed aggression. As the psychosis takes over the aggressor becomes less able to resist the hallucinations, delusions and paranoia.

Rapid cognition The ability to make very fast but accurate judgments based on very little information.

Rapid reaction skills These are the skills used to manage reactive aggression at the dysphoric tilt and require safe but reflexive responses.

Reactive aggression Aggression driven by emotion – anger, upset, annoyance, humiliation, fear, etc.

Somatosensory cortex The part of the cortex that picks up what is happening in the body.

State-dependent learning The observation that learning is recalled and reactivated in the physical, emotional and psychological states that it was learned in.

Stockholm syndrome Sometimes referred to as 'sympathy with the perpetrator' and relates to the way in which people can become attached to their abuser.

Survival schema Sets of skills that are activated in a crisis and involve no thought.

Sympathetic nervous system The part of the central nervous system activated when under threat. It is like the body's accelerator.

Thalamus The part of the brain assisted with selective attention. It selects, prior to cognition, which signals from our sensory receptors we should think about, which we should ignore, and which should activate an emergency response.

Thin-slicing Reference to the way in which it is possible to make rapid and accurate judgments based on very little information, often faster than you can think. Of course you have to 'thin-slice' the right information for processing, otherwise it's just prejudice.

Thought broadcasting A psychotic belief that others can read your thoughts and know what you are thinking.

Thought insertion A psychotic belief that others are putting thoughts into your head.

Thought withdrawal A psychotic belief that others are taking thoughts away from you.

Tonic immobility The 'freeze' state, analogous with 'playing dead' or being caught in the headlights.

Type 1 Trauma The response to recent one-off overwhelming violation, often resulting in post-traumatic stress disorder.

Type 2 Trauma The response to a ongoing continuing violation, usually in childhood, leading to complex post-traumatic stress disorder or borderline personality disorder.

Type 3 Trauma The response to many different violations over a period of time.

Under-the-radar skills Skills that seek to change behaviour without the other person being aware that their behaviour is being changed.

Word salad Reference to the jumbled conversation of someone in a psychotic state. There is a very loose association of ideas and one thought leads on to another where, to the onlooker, there is very little connection.

References

Anderson, C.A. and Bushman, B.J. (2002) Human aggression. *Annual Review of Psychology*, 53: 27–51.

Anderson, C.A. and Carnagey, N.L. (2004) Violent evil and the general aggression model. In A. Miller (ed.) *The Social Psychology of Good and Evil*. New York: Guilford Press, pp. 168–92.

Anderson, C.A. and Huesmann, L.R. (2003) Human aggression: a social-cognitive view. In M.A. Hogg and J. Cooper (eds) *Handbook of Social Psychology*. London: Sage, pp. 296–323.

Babcock, J.C., Jacobsen, N.S., Gottman, J.M. and Yerington, T.P. (2000) Attachment, emotional regulation and the function of marital violence: differences between secure, preoccupied and dismissing violent and non-violent husbands. *Journal of Family Violence*, 15: 391–9.

Bandura, A. (1977) *Social Learning Theory*. New York: Prentice Hall.

Barratt, E.S., Kent, T.A., Bryant, S.G. and Felthous, A.R. (1991) A controlled trial of phenytoin on impulsive aggression. *Journal of Clinical Psychopharmacology*, 11: 338–89.

Beck, A.T. (1999) *Prisoners of Hate*. New York: Perennial.

Behrendt, R.-P. (2006) Dysregulation of thalamic sensory 'transmission' in schizophrenia neurochemical vulnerability to hallucinations. *Journal of Psychopharmacology*, 20(3): 356–72.

Berrios, G.E. (1982) Tactile hallucinations: conceptual and historical aspects. *Journal of Neurology, Neurosurgery & Psychiatry*, 45(4): 285–93. http://www.ncbi.nlm.nih.gov/pmc/articles/PMC491362/?tool=pubmed [accessed 9 July 2012].

Berkowitz, L. (1989) Frustration-aggression hypothesis: examination and reformulation. *Psychological Bulletin*, 106: 59–73.

Berkowitz, L. (1994) Is something missing? Some observations prompted by the cognitive-neoassociationist view of anger and aggression. In L.R. Huesmann (ed.) *Aggressive Behavior: Current Perspectives*. New York: Plenum, pp. 35–7.

Björkqvist, K. and Niemlä, P. (1992) New trends in the study of female aggression. In K. Björkqvist and P. Niemlä (eds) *Of Mice and Women: Aspects of Female Aggression*. San Diego, CA: Academic Press, pp. 3–16.

Bledsoe, B.E. (2003) Critical incident stress management (CISM): benefit or risk for emergency services? *Prehospital Emergency Care*, 7(2): 272–9.

Bowers, L., Brennan, G., Winship, G. and Theodoridou, C. (2009) *Talking with Acutely Psychotic People*. http://www.iop.kcl.ac.uk/iopweb/blob/downloads/locator/l_436_Talking.pdf [accessed 9 July 2012].

Bracha, H.S. (2004) *Freeze, Flight, Fight, Fright, Faint: Adaptationist Perspectives on the Acute Stress Response Spectrum.* http://cogprints.org/5014/1/2004_C.N.S_Five_Fs_of_FEAR–Freeze_Flight_Fight_Fright_Faint.pdf [accessed 9 July 2012].

Braithwaite, R. (2001) *Managing Aggression.* Abingdon: Routledge.

Breakwell, G.M. (1997) *Coping with Aggressive Behaviour.* Leicester: BPS Books.

Brewin, C.R. (2008) What is it that a neurobiological model for PTSD must explain? *Progress in Brain Research,* 167: 217–28.

Brewin, C.R., Andrews, B. and Rose, S. (2000) Fear, helplessness, and horror in posttraumatic stress disorder: investigating *DSM-IV* Criterion A2 in victims of violent crime. *Journal of Traumatic Stress,* 13: 499–509.

Brown, A. and Bourne, I. (1996) *The Social Work Supervisor.* Buckingham: Open University Press.

Bushman, B.J., Baumeister, R.F. and Stack, A.D. (1999) Catharsis, aggression, and persuasive influence: self-fulfilling or self-defeating prophecies? *Journal of Personality and Social Psychology,* 76: 367–76.

Buss, A.H. (1961) *The Psychology of Aggression.* New York: Wiley.

David, A. (1999) On the impossibility of defining delusions. *Philosophy, Psychiatry, & Psychology,* 6(1): 17–20. http://muse.jhu.edu/login?auth=0&type=summary&url=/journals/philosophy_psychiatry_and_psychology/v006/6.1david.html [accessed 9 July 2013].

Davies, W. (2000) *Overcoming Anger and Irritability.* London: Constable & Robinson.

Davies, W. and Frude, N. (2000) *Preventing Face-to-Face Violence.* Leicester: APT Press.

De Fabrique, N., Romano, S.J., Vecchi, G.M. and Van Hasselt, V.B. (2007) *Understanding Stockholm Syndrome.* http://www.fbi.gov/stats-services/publications/law-enforcement-bulletin/2007-pdfs/july07leb.pdf [accessed 9 July 2012].

De Leon, J. and Diaz, F.J. (2005) A meta-analysis of worldwide studies demonstrates an association between schizophrenia and tobacco smoking behaviors. *Schizophrenia Research,* 76 (2–3): 135–57.

Dollard, J., Miller, N.E., Doob, L.W., Mowrer, O.H. and Sears, R.R. (1939) Adolescence. In J. Dollard, L.W. Doob, N.E. Miller, O.H. Mowrer, R.R. Sears (eds) *Frustration and Aggression.* New Haven, CT: Yale University Press, pp. 91–109.

Dyregrov, A., Solomon, R. and Bassøe, C.F. (2000) Mental mobilization processes in critical incident stress situations. *International Journal of Emergency Mental Health,* 2(2): 73–81.

Fazel, S. and Grann, M. (2006) The population impact of severe mental illness on violent crime. *American Journal of Psychiatry,* 163: 1397–403. Also available at http://ajp.psychiatryonline.org/article.aspx?articleid=96905 [accessed 9 October 2012].

Fazel, S., Gulati, G., Linsell, L., Geddes, J.R. and Grann, M. (2009) Schizophrenia and violence: systematic review and meta-analysis. *PLoS Medicine,* 6(8): e1000120. doi:10.1371/journal.pmed. 1000120 [accessed 4 October 2012].

FECYT (Spanish Foundation for Science and Technology) (2010) Empathy and violence have similar circuits in the brain, research suggests. Science Daily. http://www.sciencedaily.com/releases/2010/04/100409093405.htm [accessed 2 October 2012].

Frith, C.D. (1992) *The Cognitive Neuropsychology of Schizophrenia*. Hove: Lawrence Erlbaum.

Galanti, G. (2004) *Caring for Patients from Different Cultures*. Philadelphia, PA: University of Pennsylvania Press.

Geen, R.G. and Quanty, M.B. (1977) The catharsis of aggression: an evaluation of a hypothesis. *Advances in Experimental Social Psychology*, 10: 1–37.

Gladwell, M. (2005) *Blink: The Power of Thinking Without Thinking*. New York: Little, Brown & Co.

Gozzi, A., Jain, A., Giovanelli, A. et al. (2010) A neural switch for active and passive fear. *Neuron*, 67(4): 656–66.

Gray, J.A. (1988) *The Psychology of Fear and Stress*, 2nd edn. New York: Cambridge University Press.

Greenberg, L.S. and Safran, J.D. (1987) *Emotion in Psychotherapy*. New York: Guilford Press.

Haney, C., Banks, W.C. and Zimbardo, P.G. (1973) Interpersonal dynamics in a simulated prison. *International Journal of Criminology and Penology*, 1: 69–97.

Harrison, G. (2002) Ethnic minorities and the Mental Health Act. *The British Journal of Psychiatry*, 180: 198–9.

Hemsley, D.R. (1993) A simple (or simplistic?) cognitive model for schizophrenia. *Behaviour Research and Therapy*, 31: 633–45.

Hilton, N.Z., Harris, G.T. and Rice, M.E. (2006) Sixty-six years of research on the clinical versus actuarial prediction of violence. *The Counselling Psychologist*, 34(3): 400–9. http://psych.wfu.edu/furr/362/Clin%20vs%20act%20prediction%20of%20agg.pdf [accessed 9 July 2012].

Holtzworth-Munroe, A. (2000) A typology of men who are violent to their female partners: making sense of the heterogeneity in husband violence. *American Psychological Society*, 9: 140–3.

Huesmann, L.R. (1988) An information processing model for the development of aggression. *Aggressive Behavior*, 14: 13–24.

Keltikangas-Järvinen, L. (1982) Alexithymia in violent offenders. *Journal of Personality Assessment*, 46(5): 462–7.

Klein, G. (2004) *The Power of Intuition*. New York: Doubleday Business.

Kubany, E.S., Ralston, T.C. and Hill, E.E. (2010) Intense fear, helplessness, 'and' horror? An empirical investigation of DSM-IV PTSD criterion A2. *Psychological Trauma: Theory, Research, Practice, and Policy*, 2(2): 77–82.

Kumari, V. and Potsma, P. (2005) Nicotine use in schizophrenia: the self medication hypotheses. *Neuroscience and Biobehavioral Reviews*, 29: 1021–34. http://web.as.uky.edu/Biology/faculty/cooper/Bio401G/nicotineSchiz.pdf [accessed 9 July 2012].

LeDoux, J. (1999) *The Emotional Brain: The Mysterious Underpinnings of Emotional Life*. London: Phoenix.

LeSure-Lester, G.E. (2000) Relation between empathy and aggression and behavior compliance among abused group home youth. *Child Psychiatry Human Development*, 31(2): 153–61.

Lewin, K. (1943) Defining the 'field at a given time'. *Psychological Review*, 50: 292–310. Republished in *Resolving Social Conflicts & Field Theory in Social Science* (1997) Washington, DC: American Psychological Association.

Link, B.G., Stueve, A. and Phelan, J. (1998) Psychotic symptoms and violent behaviors: probing the components of 'threat/control-override' symptoms. *Social Psychiatry and Psychiatric Epidemiology*, 33: S55–S60.

Linsley, P. (2006) *Violence and Aggression in the Workplace*. Abingdon: Radcliffe Publishing.

Lorenz, K. (1966) *On Aggression*. New York: Harcourt Brace Jovanovich.

Mangalore, R. and Knapp, M. (2006) *Cost of Schizophrenia in England*. PSSRU Discussion Paper 2376.

McEllistrem, J. (2004) Affective and predatory violence: a bimodal classification system of human aggression and violence. *Aggression and Violent Behavior*, 10: 1–30.

Meichembaum, D. (2006) *Comparison of Aggression in Boys and Girls: A Case for Gender Specific Interventions*, available online at http://www.schoolviolenceprevention.com/meich_06_genderdifferences.pdf

Meltzer, H., Gill, B., Petticrew, M. and Hinds, K. (1995) *Surveys of Psychiatric Morbidity in Great Britain: Report 1*. London: HMSO.

Mischel, W. and Shoda, Y. (1995) A cognitive-affective system theory of personality: reconceptualizing situations, dispositions, dynamics, and invariance in personality structure. *Psychological Review*, 102: 246–68.

Monahan, J. (1981) *Predicting Violent Behavior: An Assessment of Clinical Techniques*. Beverly Hills: Sage Publications.

Monroe, R.R. (1978) *Brain Dysfunction in Aggressive Criminals*. Lexington, MA: Lexington Books.

Moya-Albiol, L., Herrero, N. and Bernal, M.C. (2010) Bases neuronales de la empatía. *Revista de Neurología*, 50(2): 89–100. Reported widely online, e.g. http://www.sciencedaily.com/releases/2010/04/100409093405.htm [accessed 9 July 2012].

Nazroo, J. and King, M. (2002) Psychosis – symptoms and estimated rates. In K. Sproston and J. Nazroo (eds) *Ethnic Minority Psychiatric Illness Rates in the Community*. London: National Centre for Social Research, TSO.

Nierhoff, D. (1999) *The Biology of Violence*. New York: The Free Press.

Perez-Alvarez, M., García-Montes, J.M., Perona-Garcelán, S. and Vallina-Fernández, O. (2008) Changing relationship with voices: new therapeutic perspectives for treating hallucinations. *Clinical Psychology and Psychotherapy*, 15: 75–85. http://members.efn.org/~ronunger/stuff/changing%20relationship%20with%20voices.pdf [accessed 9 July 2012].

Pulkkinen, L. (1987) Offensive and defensive aggression in humans: a longitudinal perspective. *Aggressive Behavior*, 13: 197–212.

Raio, C.M., Carmel, D., Carrasco, M. and Phelps, E.A. (2012) Nonconscious fear is quickly acquired but swiftly forgotten. *Current Biology*. http://www.cell.com/current-biology/fulltext/S0960-9822%2812%2900415-0 [accessed 29 August 2012].

Roth, J.A. (1994) Psychoactive substances and violence. *Research in Brief*, US Dept. of Justice. http://druglibrary.org/schaffer/GOVPUBS/psycviol.htm [accessed 9 July 2012].

Simons, D., Wurtele, S.K. and Heil, P. (2002) Childhood victimization and lack of empathy as predictors of sexual offending against women and children. *Journal of Interpersonal Violence*, 17(12): 1291–307.

Solomon, R.M. and Horn, J.M. (1986) Post-shooting traumatic reactions: a pilot study. In J. Reese and H. Goldstein (eds) *Psychological Services In Law Enforcement*. Washington, DC: United States Government Printing Office, pp. 383–93.

Walsh, E., Buchannan, A. and Fahy, T. (2002) Violence and schizophrenia: examining the evidence. *The British Journal of Psychiatry*, 180: 490–5.

Wasman, M. and Flynn, J.P. (1962) Directed attack elicited from hypothalamus. *Archives of Neurology*, 27: 635–44.

Watzlawick, P., Weakland, J. and Fisch, R. (1974) *Change*. London: W.W. Norton & Company.

Werner, P.D., Rose, T.L. and Yesavage, J.A. (1983) Reliability, accuracy and decision-making strategy in clinical predictions of imminent dangerousness. *Journal of Consulting and Clinical Psychology*, 51: 815–25.

Yerkes, R.M. and Dodson, J.D. (1908) The relationship of strength of stimulus to rapidity of habit formation. *Journal of Comparative Neurology and Psychology*, 18: 459–82.

Additional Resources

A website has been set up to support this book and can be found at www.facingdanger.com

There you will find links to resources that relate to the various issues raised in each chapter and these will be continually updated.

Additionally you will find details of how to stay in contact through Twitter, Facebook, LinkedIn and our blog at Wordpress.

If you are interested in the training that this book is based upon, you can find details at www.dangerousbehaviour.com or you can email me directly at impact@dangerous behaviour.com

Index